"Useful for anyone interested in sexuality and gender, the process of interviewing is assessed at the micro level which shines a light on complex personal dynamics. Using case studies to illuminate the nature of the interviewer–participant encounter, this reflective account provides an intimate expose of an area of methodology which is rarely discussed. A must for anyone planning or doing sensitive interviewing".

Teela Sanders, *Professor of Criminology, University of Leicester, UK*

A CRITICAL REFLEXIVE APPROACH TO SEX RESEARCH

A Critical Reflexive Approach to Sex Research is a methodologically focused book that offers rich insights into the, often secret, subjectivities of men who pay for sex in South Africa. The book centres on the interview context, outlining a critical reflexive approach to understanding how knowledge is co-produced by both the interviewer and the participant in research about sex.

By attending to the complex dynamics of the research interview, this book examines the historic and contemporary relationship between sex work, race, coloniality, sexuality, masculinity, femininity, whorephobia, and discourses of disease and contagion. It draws on both empirical interview data and Huysamen's entries in her research journal to offer a unique approach to building critical reflexivity into every phase of the research process. The critical reflexive approach uses an assemblage of poststructuralist and psychoanalytic theories and practices which together provide tools to interrogate how interview dynamics facilitate, shape, and restrain the meaning that is produced within the interview. This book will be a valuable resource for anyone interested in researching sex work from intersectional and feminist decolonial perspectives as it probes critical questions surrounding how men make meaning of paying for sex, their motivations for doing so, and how they negotiate their identities in relation to this stigmatised practice. It provides a unique offering to researchers working on sexual, secret, and stigmatised topics, providing them with a specific set of tools and resources to incorporate reflexivity into their own sex research.

Encouraging the reader to look widely to draw on an array of theories and frameworks across disciplines, this is fascinating reading for students and researchers in critical psychology, research methods, and the social sciences.

Monique Huysamen, PhD, is a researcher at Manchester Metropolitan University. She received her PhD in Psychology from the University of Cape Town, where she now holds an honorary research position. Her research focuses on sexualities, sexual health, and social justice. She has also published on research ethics and critical approaches to doing qualitative research.

Concepts for Critical Psychology: Disciplinary Boundaries Re-thought

Series editor: Ian Parker

Developments inside psychology that question the history of the discipline and the way it functions in society have led many psychologists to look outside the discipline for new ideas. This series draws on cutting edge critiques from just outside psychology in order to complement and question critical arguments emerging inside. The authors provide new perspectives on subjectivity from disciplinary debates and cultural phenomena adjacent to traditional studies of the individual.

The books in the series are useful for advanced level undergraduate and postgraduate students, researchers and lecturers in psychology and other related disciplines such as cultural studies, geography, literary theory, philosophy, psychotherapy, social work and sociology.

Most recently published titles:

A Critical Reflexive Approach to Sex Research
Interviews with Men Who Pay for Sex
Monique Huysamen

Psychology, Punitive Activation and Welfare
Blaming the Unemployed
Rose-Marie Stambe

For more information about this series, please visit: www.routledge.com

A CRITICAL REFLEXIVE APPROACH TO SEX RESEARCH

Interviews with Men Who Pay for Sex

Monique Huysamen

Routledge
Taylor & Francis Group

LONDON AND NEW YORK

Cover image: © Getty Images

First published 2022
by Routledge
4 Park Square, Milton Park, Abingdon, Oxon OX14 4RN

and by Routledge
605 Third Avenue, New York, NY 10158

Routledge is an imprint of the Taylor & Francis Group, an informa business

British Library Cataloguing-in-Publication Data
A catalogue record for this book is available from the British Library

Library of Congress Cataloging-in-Publication Data
A catalog record for this book has been requested

ISBN: 978-0-367-62377-7 (hbk)
ISBN: 978-0-367-55447-7 (pbk)
ISBN: 978-1-003-09360-2 (ebk)

DOI: 10.4324/9781003093602

Typeset in Bembo
by Apex CoVantage, LLC

CONTENTS

ACKNOWLEDGEMENTS

I would like to thank:

Foremost, my partner, Liam Stowell.

Professor Floretta Boonzaier and the Hub for Decolonial Feminist Psychology in Africa for supervising this research and for instilling the research values and principles upon which this book is based.

Professor Ian Parker and Professor Erica Burman for your support with this book and for building a community of learning, support, and solidarity through spaces like the Discourse Unit and Discourse Unplugged, from which many of us benefit.

The Department of Social Care and Social Work at Manchester Metropolitan University for supporting me with an invaluable resource, time, to write this book.

Professor David Gadd.

Professor Teela Sanders.

Professor Rob Pattman.

Professor Julie Barnett.

Professor Chris Hatton.

Terry Dowdall.

Erin Coe and Jade Taylor Cooke.

Dr Jaime García-Iglesias, Chapter 4 is for you.

My mum and dad, Noela and Deon Huysamen.

My funders: the Harry Crossley Foundation, the National Research Foundation (NRF), the Commonwealth Scholarship Commission (CSC), and the University of Cape Town.

SERIES PREFACE FOR MONIQUE HUYSAMEN'S *A CRITICAL REFLEXIVE APPROACH TO SEX RESEARCH: INTERVIEWS WITH MEN WHO PAY FOR SEX*

This book pushes at the "reflexivity" that is claimed by so many psychologists now – an earnest well-meaning attempt to tell us more about what is going on in the background of a publication – and shows the limits of that. The limited standard response of supervisors of projects and dissertations looking for reflexivity is to ask for an additional "reflexive analysis" in which we might learn about the personal trajectory of the researcher and perhaps have an account of who they are, what they thought, and what they felt. That is, as a complement to the assessment of the work – the disciplinary surveillance aspect of academic and professional practice – there is a demand that the writer tell us more about themselves, to configure themselves in the trap of confession.

The further, deeper, more radical reflexive turn elaborated in this book, in contrast, elaborates a "critical reflexive approach", doing so in a context that exactly demands that questions of context, institution, and power are put to the forefront. In place of personal individualised reflexivity and all of the psychologised paraphernalia that the discipline has now come to expect from qualitative research, we need to focus on what might be termed "institutional reflexivity". It is this reflexive approach that is critical, and which Monique Huysamen shows us must be intersectional; then we can work with subjectivity, locating it instead of reducing everything else to it.

Every interview context is "difficult", but these difficulties are too-often smoothed over, smoothed into the illusory claim that "rapport" was established between interviewer and interviewee, and so the reader can be confident that information was freely given, accurately transcribed, and can now be "understood". Every version of discourse analysis tells us otherwise, shows us how the text, every text, is artfully constructed, and constructed out of available resources that frame and mislead the reader while indeed giving them the illusion of understanding what really went on and, if the interviewer is smart enough, the illusion of understanding what went on inside the interviewee's head.

These difficulties are foregrounded in this book that is in line with discourse-analytic sensitivity to the construction of text, designed to shake us from these illusions and make us face what is going on, how subjectivity itself is fabricated. That subjectivity, which is the touchstone of humanist qualitative research, is actually always pieced together. Here, with sex and "race" so evident as contextual-cultural framing of what is said and what is "understood", that discourse-analytic sensitivity needs to take an explicitly intersectional approach, theorising how sex is stigmatised and enabling us to decolonise the accounts and the process and the very relationships that are constructed and challenged in the course of the interviews.

This book not only embeds reflexivity in this sex research but also shows us how reflexivity must be embedded in every piece of good research. It gives us a standpoint, many intersectionally aware standpoints from which to view power and the construction of subjectivity, standpoints that do not pretend to be "outside" the interview process but are precisely so telling because they are an intimate part of that process. It is inside and outside simultaneously, "outwith" the interview as a tool of research, and "outwith" psychology as such.

Ian Parker
University of Manchester

1

SETTING THE SCENE

Researching men who pay for sex in South Africa

Arriving at the research

As a doctoral student I, a white woman in my twenties, interviewed 43 cisgender men who pay women for sex in South Africa, a country where sex work is criminalised and stigmatised. This methodologically focused book is about my research process. But, as I will discuss throughout this book, research is about arrivals of various kinds, and I arrived at the study and the approach outlined in this book via an earlier research encounter. As a Master's student, I set out to interview men who had paid for sex in Cape Town. I hoped to uncover their motivations for paying for sex and explore how these motivations were connected to broader questions of men and masculinities, intimacy, and sexuality in post-apartheid South Africa. Indeed, the interviews did offer important insights into these questions (see Huysamen & Boonzaier, 2015). But it was after these interviews were completed, as I sat down to analyse the transcripts, that I was first struck by significance of the interviewer–participant dynamics. As I thought more about the interviews – about what was said, what was not said, how it was said, by whom, and to what ends – I was struck by the complex and powerful ways that the interview relationship influenced my research findings (see Huysamen, 2016). I became more and more interested in how the dynamics occurring inside the interview encounter provided crucial insights into participants' lives outside that encounter and about how participants managed and negotiated their identities in relation to this stigmatised sexual

DOI: 10.4324/9781003093602-1

practice. I wished that I had more intentionally and systematically captured these important dynamics at every stage of the research process, rather than just trying to reflect and write about them after the fact. This prompted the design of the present study, in which I aimed to develop an approach which would allow me to foreground and interrogate these fascinating interview relationships and the role that they played in shaping the research. This book is the result of that project. In its pages, I outline the critical reflexive approach which enabled me to build reflexivity into the fabric of my research design.

This is a methodological book in so far as I lay out the combination of principles, philosophies, approaches, and techniques that I used to build critical reflexivity into the research design. The book draws on both the empirical interview data and my reflections of the research process to present a critical reflexive approach to engaging in qualitative research around topics that are of a sexual, secretive, or stigmatised nature. It also offers in-depth insights into the subjectivities of men who pay for sex, exploring questions around men's motivation for paying for sex, and their identity construction. The critical reflexive approach outlined in this book is neither a step-by-step research guide, nor are the individual components of which it is comprised novel. Rather the critical reflexive approach is an assemblage of well-established theoretical and methodological frameworks and approaches drawn from poststructuralist and psychoanalytic thought which can be used together to build reflexivity into the research design with the intention of deepening the theoretical insights into the topics we study. The intention is that, by the end of this book, the reader should have ideas about how they can adapt and apply some of these insights, methods, and tools to their own research processes.

As qualitative researchers, we know that reflexive practices are important because they provide an opportunity for building both rigour and transparency into our research design. However, my central argument in this book is that attending to these seemingly methodological aspects of interviews is also *theoretically* generative. Attending to interviewer–participant dynamics as they unfold in the interview encounter is not only important because it offers insight in our research design, but also because it will provide deeper and more nuanced insight into our research topics and into our participants' subjectivities. Thus, true to this central principle, each chapter in this book is structured around methodological themes but will also tell you something new about men's motivations for paying for sex and how they managed and negotiated these client identities.

Paying for sex in context: representations of sex work in South Africa

What does it mean to pay for sex in South Africa?[1] The ways in which sex work and those who engage with the industry are positioned by and within South African society is directly and deeply connected to how participants in this study felt about paying for sex, to their motivations for participating in the study, to how participants positioned themselves in interviews, to where and how the interviews took place, and to how I related and responded to participants in interviews. These broader social meanings of sex work (or of any issue we study, for that matter) form part of the conditions under which our participants arrive to take part in our research and form a crucial part of the interview context. To highlight the importance of understanding sex work in context, Zatz argues that,

> It is quite common to talk glibly of prostitution as the world's oldest profession, existing universally across time and place. Such talk obscures the differences in the social and cultural context – differences in economic organization, normative sexual practices, and the relationship between sexual practices and identity, between economic practices and identity, and so on – that shape the significance and structure of prostitution within any particular historical space.
>
> *(Zatz, 1997, p. 278)*

Men who pay for sex in South Africa do so in the context of an unequal society where sex work is highly stigmatised and fully criminalised. All persons engaged in sex work – buyer, seller, and third parties – are criminalised under South African law (Richter et al., 2020). Criminalisation creates a context which not only stigmatises people who participate in sex work but also significantly increases the risk of violence and health-related risks involved (Platt et al., 2018). In South Africa, sex work is complicated by high national levels of unemployment, some of the highest rates of gender-based violence in the world, crippling poverty, and a national HIV/AIDS epidemic (South African Law Reform Commission, 2017).

The stigmatisation of sex work in South African society is far from unique, people involved in sex work remain stigmatised, to varying degrees, throughout the world (Levine, 2003; Sanders & Campbell, 2008; Smith & Mac, 2018; Weitzer, 2018). A rise in antitrafficking ideology internationally has seen sex work increasingly conflated with sex trafficking, increasing moral panic around sex work in many contexts. The onset of the coronavirus pandemic early in 2020 further stoked public discussions about sex workers as "vectors of disease" in many parts of the world. But in South Africa, where legal and academic discourses continue to position sex workers and their clients as criminals and as responsible for the spread of HIV/AIDS, the public panic and disgust in relation to sex work is exacerbated.

Sex work and discourses of dirt and disease: a historically informed account

An intersectional and historically informed understanding of sex work in South Africa is crucial for engaging with men's narratives about paying for sex that are presented throughout this book. Sex work has a long history as a stigmatised practice in South Africa. Since the colonial era, sex work has been associated with discourses of disease, contagion, and moral decay. These discourses have repeatedly filtered into public policy and legislation, where they have intensified public panic about sex work and have been used to justify extending state control over sex workers (Huysamen & Boonzaier, 2018; Van Heyningen, 1984). For example, in an analysis of how women's bodies were portrayed in nineteenth-century art, medicine, and literature, Gilman (1985) shows how "the prostitute" was constructed as the essentially sexualised woman associated with moral corruption, physical pathology, disease, and societal decay. Similarly, Levine (2003), in an archival case study of British colonial policies around "prostitution" and venereal disease, shows that between 1850 and 1880, virtually every British colony, including the Cape Colony in South Africa, was subject to contagious disease regulations that identified "prostitutes" as the primary source of contagion. The Contagious Diseases Act was passed in the Cape Colony in 1868 to "protect" British armed forces from venereal disease. This legislation identified prostitutes as the primary source of sexually transmitted disease and allowed police officers to arrest women who were suspected of being prostitutes, subject them to invasive checks for sexually transmitted infections, and then confine them to hospitals for up to three months (Gilman, 1985; Levine, 2003; Van Heyningen, 1984).

These colonial understandings of sex workers as vectors of disease persist in contemporary South Africa, which continues to face the largest HIV epidemic in the world (Huysamen & Boonzaier, 2018). Sex workers are identified in public health policy as a "key population" that are greatly affected by HIV (UNAIDS, 2016). This recognition is very important for shaping the South African government's HIV response and ensuring that sex worker's sexual health needs are prioritised. However, sex work is also stigmatised by this association with the spread of HIV (Lawless et al., 1996). Clients of sex workers are also increasingly being associated with the spread of HIV, and recent research suggests that clients of sex workers play "a fundamental role in HIV transmission" in South Africa (Stone et al., 2021, p. 1). Much social science research on both clients and sex workers has focused on HIV risk-taking behaviours and gender-based violence (Karim et al., 1995; McKeganey, 1994; Stadler & Delany, 2006; Townsend et al., 2011; Wojcicki & Malala, 2001).

Discourses linking sex work to disease and contagion have real-world policy implications that reach beyond informing the South African government's public health funding strategies and responses. They are also currently used in arguments to support the continuation of the full criminalisation of sex work under the Criminal Law Sexual Offences and Related Matters Amendment Act 32 of 2007, also known as the Sexual Offences Act (South African Law Reform Commission, 2017). Like the colonial-era legislation, the Sexual Offences Act grants the police the power to search and arrest sex workers at their discretion (Richter & Bodin, 2017). Unsurprisingly, this legal position makes sex workers vulnerable. Research consistently shows that sex workers experience physical and sexual violence and human rights violations at the hands of police (Evans et al., 2019; Wojcicki & Malala, 2001). The full criminalisation of sex work in turn feeds into and fuels moral panic and public condemnation of sex workers and their clients. This creates a cycle that is extremely difficult to break. Thus, long-held understandings of sex work as a public health risk, a threat to the traditional family unit, and a cause of the moral decay of South African society remain pervasive (Gardner, 2009).

In South Africa, sex work is often over simplified and conflated with human trafficking despite a lack of clear evidence to support this assertion, allowing migrant sex workers to be constructed as inevitable victims of trafficking and clients as morally corrupt people who support human trafficking (Yingwana et al., 2019). Simultaneously, arguments for the decriminalisation of sex work are discounted due to claims about the risks of increased trafficking (Yingwana et al., 2019). The criminalisation of sex work in South Africa persists despite decades of tireless lobbying and advocacy for decriminalisation (Amnesty International, 2016; Mgbako, 2016; Richter & Bodin, 2017) and empirical research evidencing that the criminalisation of sex work harms sex workers (Platt et al., 2018). Alternative discourses that move beyond this moral panic to acknowledge sex work as a legitimate form of work exist and inform the push for decriminalisation. However, in a society where buying and selling sex remains a criminal offence, these ideas about sex work remain relatively marginal (Richter et al., 2020).

In South Africa, the close relationship between sex work, dirt, disease, and moral corruption is deeply complicated by both race and class (Huysamen & Boonzaier, 2018). It has been more than two decades since South Africa's transition from apartheid to a constitutional democracy in 1994, yet South Africa remains one of the most economically unequal societies in the world (Richter et al., 2020). Poverty and inequality in South Africa are strongly correlated with race and gender: the most marginalised members of society are black women (Statistics South Africa, 2017). It is thus not surprising that the majority of the poorest street-based sex workers are black women (Gould, 2014; Mgbako, 2016).

Not all sex workers are equally disadvantaged by the stigmatisation and criminalisation of sex work. Levine (2003, p. 2) argues that laws that criminalise sex workers have throughout history punished poor working-class sex workers operating in visible contexts, for example, streets, while "drawing a veil over the more discreet and hidden forms of sexual servicing exclusive to the wealthy". In contemporary South Africa, it is primarily poor black sex workers who bear the brunt of the laws and its associated stigma. By contrast, sex workers in better economic positions working from discreet indoor settings are often less directly affected by this stigma and its legal repercussions. Poor black women selling sex outdoors are more visible to the public, more stigmatised in their communities, more vulnerable to gender-based violence, and more likely to be targeted by the police. It is the black woman's body that continues to be devalued (see Boonzaier, 2017) and read through the lenses of dirt and disease.

The image of the black woman sex worker's body as a vector for disease in turn feeds into broader, long-held colonial tropes of the black body as dirty and diseased and in need of management and control. Zoia (2015), in his thesis, *Sanitizing South Africa: Race, racism and germs in the making of the Apartheid state, 1880–1980*, shows how the emergence of germ theory and sanitisation discourses during the late-nineteenth century encouraged black African bodies to be constructed as dirty and diseased in relation to white bodies, which were valorised and defined in terms of purity, sanitisation, and the absence of disease:

> Occurring at a time when the British Empire was at its zenith, it would be the black body that was to assume the role of principal germ-carrier for the white colonists could certainly not blame their (imagined to be) superior selves for epidemic disease. Racism then resulted when a sense of disgust came to characterize white encounters with said black body; a sense of disgust that was given public legitimacy through the science and social science of the first half of the Twentieth Century that reified racial difference as natural and unchanging.
>
> *(Zoia, 2015, p. 158)*

These imaginaries of "dirty" and "diseased" black bodies are still very much present in post-colonial, post-apartheid South Africa, and are also given public and scientific legitimacy through biomedical HIV/AIDS discourses. For example, Patton (1990) discusses how colonial constructions of black sexuality have been revived in efforts to explain the characteristics of the AIDS epidemic. Thus, we see a recurring pattern: the policies that criminalise sex work and discourses that associate women sex workers with contemporary concerns about disease contribute to maintaining stigmatised understandings of sex work *and* the dominance of colonial tropes about the black body. This highlights the circular and interlocking nature of the relationship between representations and experiences of sex work, gender, class, race, and the law. Colonial understandings of sex work in terms of contamination, dirt, and disease are reflected in contemporary discourses about state responses to sex work, while these associations of dirt and disease actively work to reproduce the colonial invention of the black women's body as Other. This demonstrates how coloniality, race class, gender, and sexuality not only intersect but also are fused and continue to shape the meaning and representations of sex work in South Africa. It is within this complex context that men like the participants in my study pay for sex. It is against this backdrop of stigma, criminalisation, and public condemnation of sex work that they make meaning of paying for sex and must negotiate their identities.

An introduction to men who pay for sex

What do we think of when we think about men who pay for sex? In addition to "clients", terms like "Johns", "tricks", "punters", and "kerbcrawlers" are used in different contexts to refer to men who pay for sex. Many of these terms tend to conjure up one of several stigmatised tropes about men who pay for sex, and public understandings of clients as "perverted", "hypersexual", "dangerous", "deviant", "socially inept", "desperate", "violent", "diseased", and "exploitative" are all quite common. These rather derogatory stereotypes assume that all men who pay for sex do so either because they are hypersexual, perverted, or predatory, or because they are socially or physically unable to access sex otherwise. In South Africa, which has one of the highest rates of gender-based violence in the world, and where sex workers do experience high rates of violence at the hands of men, including clients, the police, and their intimate partners, men who pay for sex are often imagined as violent and exploitative and "part of the problem" of gender-based violence.

The ways in which a particular country or jurisdiction legislates sex work and how their public health and social policies respond to clients both reflects and can play a large role in shaping how clients are understood in that society. Client intervention programmes are one such example. While there is almost no published work on client intervention programmes in South Africa (see Huysamen & Richter, 2020), the most well-known client interventions are the "John School" re-education programmes, which were first started in the United States in the 1990s, and the "kerbcrawler" rehabilitation programmes in the United Kingdom, aimed at men soliciting sex on the street. These one-day diversionary programmes for men who have been convicted of "soliciting prostitution" are administered through the country's criminal justice system with the aim of reducing the number of men who pay for sex. These programmes are based on (and at the same time reinforce) stereotyped understandings of sex work as inherently harmful and of clients as inherently deviant men who need to be "reformed", "re-educated", and "rehabilitated" into society (Sanders, 2009; van Brunschot, 2003).

Sanders (2012), in her book *Paying for Pleasure: Men Who Pay for Sex*, offers a pertinent example of how stereotyped understandings of clients are reproduced in public discourse in the United Kingdom. She presents a leaflet from a campaign by the police in Wolverhampton (part of the West Midlands Police Force). The leaflet (see BBC News, 2006) depicts an image of a man's face looking up from a dark sewer through "bars" of a drain cover at road level, as though imprisoned by them. The accompanying text reads, "Kerb-crawlers end up behind bars: Wolverhampton hates kerb-crawling. So, get out and stay out!" This campaign material conjures up the image of the client who solicits sex from the street as someone who is literally and symbolically in the "gutter", a criminal who should be "behind bars". The leaflet's wording positions men who pay for sex as though they are not part of the Wolverhampton community, as Other, and as a threat to a community who despise them. Such depictions of clients from the Global North filter into news, film, and popular media and influence how men who pay for sex across the world are understood and how they themselves make meaning of paying for sex. Indeed, Prior and Peled (2021, p. 724) reviewed all research published about men who pay for sex and their identity construction over the past 20 years. Their findings confirm that the stigma associated with paying for sex permeates many spheres of men's lives and "affects their gendered, sexual, cultural, intimate, consumerist, and social identities and self-perceptions".

Perhaps it may seem as though I have painted and exaggerated an overly bleak picture of how men who pay for sex are imagined and represented. Of course, not all people think of men who pay for sex in this way, but these are tropes that are commonly associated with clients. These caricatures of the client are significant to the current study because they followed participants to the interview and were part of the unspoken context of interviews. Participants arrived at interviews having to negotiate their identities in response to the implicit stereotypes and negative versions of masculinity associated with men who pay for sex. Indeed, much of this book is about how men managed and defended their identities in the face of this stigma.

Who are the men who pay for sex?

Sex is bought and sold by people of every gender and sexual identity. However, research suggests that cisgender men are the primary purchasers of sex and cisgender women remain the primary sellers of sex

(Smith & Mac, 2018). In the present study, I interviewed cisgender men who identified as ever having paid women for sex. While there is a well-established and growing body of literature about sex workers' experiences in South Africa (e.g. Gould & Fick, 2008; Richter et al., 2014; Scorgie et al., 2013; Stadler & Delany, 2006; Yingwana et al., 2019), we know comparatively little about men who pay for sex. With a few exceptions (e.g. Huschke & Coetzee, 2019; Huysamen, 2020; Jewkes et al., 2012a, 2012b; Trotter, 2008), most research on clients has been conducted outside of South Africa (Brents et al., 2020; Hammond & Hooff, 2019; Prior & Peled, 2019; Sanders et al., 2020).

A substantial proportion of this international research on clients endeavours to profile men who pay for sex into prototypical client groups, according to socio-demographic variables such as age, marital status, education level, and class (Belza et al., 2008; Monto & McRee, 2005; Pitts et al., 2004; Xantidis & McCabe, 2000). However, the findings of these studies tend to be largely contradictory, and examining the results collectively suggests that men who pay for sex are not a homogenous group who can be easily categorised (Huysamen, 2020; Monto, 2004). Rather, in-depth qualitative research suggests that men from all walks of life pay for sex for a variety of reasons that may change throughout their lives (Huschke & Schubotz, 2016; Huysamen, 2019; Prior & Peled, 2019; Sanders, 2012).

My experience researching sex work in South Africa for more than a decade suggests that men of every socio-economic status, from the very rich and affluent to those who are poor and marginalised, pay for sex. During my time researching men who pay for sex, I have interviewed clients who are high-powered businessmen; professionals like engineers, lawyers, and bankers; police officers; healthcare workers; long-haul truck drivers; people working in creative industries; people who own their own business; and people who are precariously employed or are unemployed. My research experience suggests that men of all races and religious and non-religious backgrounds pay for sex in South Africa. Men who are single, married, engaged, and in open relationships pay for sex. Many men choose to pay for sex instead of, or in addition to, other available options. Some men who are physically disabled pay for sex. Some men who are neurodivergent pay for sex. Some clients have self-reported using violence against women in interviews (Jewkes et al., 2012b, 2012a), but others have explicitly distanced themselves from violence and describe themselves as non-violent and respectful men (Huysamen,

2016). In South Africa, men solicit and have sex they have paid for in various contexts, including online, in taverns, in brothels, in high-end "adult entertainment" clubs, on busy streets in the city, at the entrances to farms in agricultural areas, at truck-stops, near shipping docks, on the outskirts of townships and informal settlements, in their family homes, in sex workers' private residences, in hotels, and just about anywhere else it is possible to meet to have sex. There is no one prototypical sex work client, and the "types" of clients that you meet are likely to be directly related to how and where you look for them. But more about this in Chapter 2, where I introduce the men who arrived to participate in the current study.

What motivates men to pay for sex?

Men who pay for sex are not homogenous, and neither are their reasons for paying. However, research suggests that dominant heteronormative ideas about both masculinity and femininity tend to filter into and shape the meanings that cisgender men make of paying women for sex (Hammond & Hooff, 2019; Huysamen, 2020; Huysamen & Boonzaier, 2015; Prior & Peled, 2021; Sanders, 2012). For example, some men who pay for sex draw on the sex drive discourse (Hollway, 2001), the idea that men have an inherent and urgent biological need for sex, to articulate their motivations for paying for sex. They understand sex as something that men need, and they see paying for it as a straightforward way to get the sex they want, when they want it (Hammond & Hooff, 2019). Many men speak about the "no strings attached" or "sex without responsibility" benefit of paying for sex (Bernstein, 2007; Hammond & Hooff, 2019; Huysamen & Boonzaier, 2015; Plumridge et al., 1997). Some men suggest that the clear contractual agreement between client and sex worker involves less work and fuss and can cost them less than meeting someone in bar for a causal encounter, where there are certain flirting scripts or dating etiquette to follow, such as paying for drinks and getting to know one another.

Men's "no strings attached" narratives about paying for sex are often motivated by dominant patriarchal understandings of women's sexuality where women are imagined as "needy" and as only using casual sex to "catch a man" and secure long-term committed relationships. These tropes ignore the fact women may seek no strings attached casual sex for pleasure and enjoyment too (Bareket et al., 2018; Hollway, 2001).

Paid sex is desirable to some men because it allows them to fulfil their "need" for sex, while the monetary exchange absolves them from any of the obligations, responsibilities, or negative aspects commonly associated with women in heterosexual relationships (Bernstein, 2007). For some men who seek sexual encounters outside of their marriages, the "no strings attached" bounded nature of paid sex is particularly important to ensure that these sexual encounters remain separate from their marriages. Some men who are unsatisfied with their sexual relationships with their wives even suggest that paying for sex (rather than having an affair or leaving their wives) saves their marriages and the family unit (Hammond & Hooff, 2019; Huysamen & Boonzaier, 2015).

Some men pay for sex in pursuit of the excitement, the thrill, and the element of risk (Birch & Ireland, 2015). Others seek the variety and diversity of sexual partners and experiences that paying for sex affords them (Joseph & Black, 2012; Xantidis & McCabe, 2000). Some married men say that they pay for sex because the kind of "porn star" sex they pay for is fundamentally different to the more mundane and conservative sex that they have with their wives (Huysamen, 2020; Huysamen & Boonzaier, 2015). This feeds into the binary ways in which women and their sexualities are constructed as either promiscuous whore figures or respectable wife figures (Bareket et al., 2018) (more on this in Chapter 3). Research about men who participate in sex tourism suggests that these men travel to foreign countries (usually in the Global South) specifically in pursuit of difference, to have sex with "exotic" local women (Brennan, 2001; Garrick, 2005; Katsulis, 2010; O'Connell Davidson, 2000). The eroticisation of the exotic cultural Other tends to be overt in these men's accounts.

Critical qualitative research on masculinities shows how dominant heteronormative constructions of male sexuality are centred on the notion of sexual "performance" and skill (Farvid & Braun, 2006; Potts, 2000b). This is the idea that the ideal man is sexually experienced, skilled, virile, confident, ever-ready for sex, and able to attract multiple sexual partners and always bring women to orgasm, as evidence of this skill (Potts, 2000a, 2000b). These largely unrealistic and uninhabitable versions of male sexuality are often implicated in men's motivations for paying for sex. When they feel their own sexual experiences, relationships, or "performances" do not match up to these ideals, some men seek out paid sexual encounters (Huysamen, 2020). Paid sexual encounters with an experienced and patient sex worker means men can experiment with different kinds of sex and develop new sexual skills that allow them to better approximate these idealised versions of masculinity. Precisely because men are "paying for it", paid sexual encounters provide a safe space where men feel less judged and even exempt from some of the expectations to "perform" sexually (Frank, 2003). They can have sex without having to worry about exposing sexual dysfunction or inadequacies they may feel they have (Huysamen, 2020). For some men, their first paid sexual encounters are also their first sexual encounters, and they pay for sex as a way to "lose" their virginity and the sexual inexperience that it represents (Hammond & Hooff, 2019; Huysamen, 2020; Joseph & Black, 2012). Experienced non-judgemental sex workers provide an environment where these men do not have to worry about getting it wrong, making a fool of themselves, or being rejected. Some men in heterosexual relationships also use paid sexual encounters as a safe and shame-free environment to explore their sexual identities and their desires that fall outside of the norms of compulsory heterosexuality (Huysamen, 2019). This shows that men use these paid encounters as more than just places to "get sex" and speaks to some of the emotional demands that men place on their paid sexual encounters (Hoang, 2010; Sanders, 2012).

While men often talk about how paying for sex offers "porn star sex", variety, and "no strings attached sex", very often the same men also speak about their desire for closeness, intimacy, and connection in their paid sexual encounters. They describe these as aspects as missing from the other intimate relationships in their lives. In fact, men's desire for intimacy and emotional connection and closeness in paid sexual encounters is one of the most common and central themes to emerge from qualitative research on men who pay for sex (Hammond & Hooff, 2019; Huschke & Schubotz, 2016; Huysamen, 2020; Huysamen & Boonzaier, 2015; Sanders, 2008, 2012). As Sanders (2008, p. 413) writes, "the sex industry is not simply about selling sex and sexual fantasies" – it is also about attending to the emotional needs of clients. Gezinski et al. (2016, p. 792) argue that men seek out paid sexual encounters that allow them to "imagine themselves as seen, chosen, and desired". For many men, the more the client – sex worker interaction resembles an authentic romantic encounter, the more satisfactory it is. This kind of "authenticity" is often referred to as the "girlfriend experience" (Bernstein, 2007; Chen, 2005; Huff, 2011; Milrod & Monto, 2012). Rather than having sex with women who were "clock-watching" and seemed indifferent and disinterested, men want to feel that women they pay for sex are genuinely engaged and derive pleasure and enjoyment from the experience with them (Bernstein, 2007; Chen, 2005; Holzman & Pines, 1982; Milrod & Monto, 2012; Sanders, 2008).

Clients and sex workers who see one another over a long period of time can and do build genuine connections and emotional ties (Kong, 2015; Sanders, 2012). However, research repeatedly shows that most men are aware that that intimacy and emotionality involved in paid sex is generally time-limited, restricted to the time spent together during the paid encounter, and often to some extent manufactured or performed (Bernstein, 2007). For example, a participant in a study with men who pay for sex in Cape Town says, "you see a lot of those girls are so good they make a guy believe, for that hour, that he is it. He is just Mr Hunk himself", acknowledging the time-limited and bounded nature of the interaction (Huysamen & Boonzaier, 2015, p. 548). Bernstein (2007) argues that it is precisely this "bounded authenticity", the fact that paying for sex provides the intimacy of a genuine relationship but within boundaries that insulate them from the obligations and complications commonly associated with hetero-sexual relationships, that makes paying for sex appealing to many men.

This section represents merely a snapshot of some of the academic research on men's motivations for paying for sex. What it demonstrates is that men pay for sex for a variety of reasons, and these reasons are shaped by the imperatives of dominant understandings of masculinity, feminin-ity, and heterosexuality. While setting out the key tenets of the critical reflexive approach, the chapters that follow will build on this body of research by offering insight into why the men who participated in my study pay for sex; how the meanings they make of paying for sex are shaped by race, class, and coloniality; and how they managed their iden-tities in relation to the stigma of being a sex work client in South Africa.

Outline of the book

This chapter has set the scene for the rest of the book by discuss-ing the motivations behind the book and introducing the context of paying for sex in South Africa. Chapter 2 provides a theoretical framing for the critical reflexive approach presented in this book and outlines the methods used in my study. Chapter 3 foregrounds the significance of attending to the question of "arrivals" in research. I demonstrate how exploring participants' motivations for arriving to interviews about paying for sex provided insights into, and often mirrored, their motivations for paying for sex. Drawing on excerpts from interviews and from my own reflective journal, Chapter 4 examines a central assumption of the critical reflexive approach: the interviewer and the participant are defended and sexual subjects who bring their defences and desires to interviews about sex, and that these defences and desires penetrate the interview relationship and shape the data that are produced there. In Chapter 5, I apply intersectionality and feminist decolonial theories to my reflexive practice to interrogate how race, class, gender, and sexuality operated together within the interview relationship to shape the meanings produced there. This chapter demonstrates how men deployed racist and colonial discourses to manage and defend against the stigma associated with sex work in South Africa and explores the possibilities for using critical reflexivity as a tool for decolonial research practice. Chapter 6 concludes by outlining the nine core elements that make up the foundations of the critical reflexive approach presented in this book. I invite the readers to imagine how these might be adapted to build critical reflexivity into their own research about sexual, secret, or stigmatised topics.

Note

1 Sex work is an issue around which feminists remain vehemently divided. While there is not enough space for detailed discussion on the long-standing and continuing debates within the broad church of feminism surrounding sex work in this book, thorough discussions and analyses of these debates are presented elsewhere (see Hewer, 2021; Huysamen, 2017; Mgbako, 2016; Smith & Mac, 2018; Zatz, 1997).

References

Amnesty International. (2016). *Policy on state obligations to respect, protect, and fulfil the human rights of sex workers.* Policy 30/4063/2016. www.amnesty. org/en/documents/pol30/4062/2016/en/

Bareket, O., Kahalon, R., Shnabel, N., & Glick, P. (2018). The Madonna-Whore dichotomy: Men who perceive women's nurturance and sexuality as mutually exclusive endorse patriarchy and show lower relationship satisfaction. *Sex Roles, 79*(9), 519–532. https://doi.org/10.1007/s11199-018-0895-7

BBC News. (2006, February 21). Posters target city kerb crawlers. *BBC News.* http://news.bbc.co.uk/1/hi/england/west_midlands/4736892.stm

Belza, M. J., Fuente, L. de la, Suárez, M., Vallejo, F., García, M., López, M., Barrio, G., Bolea, Á., & Group, T. H. A. S. B. S. (2008). Men who pay for sex in Spain and condom use: Prevalence and correlates in a representative sample of the general population. *Sexually Transmitted Infections, 84*(3), 207–211.

Bernstein, E. (2007). Sex work for the middle classes. *Sexualities, 10*(4), 473–488.

Birch, P., & Ireland, J. (2015). Men procuring sexual services from women: Everyman or peculiar man? *Journal of Forensic Practice, 17*(1), 13–20. https://doi.org/10.1108/JFP-03-2014-0007

Boonzaier, F. (2017). The life and death of Anene Booysen: Colonial discourse, gender-based violence and media representations. *South African Journal of Psychology, 47*(4), 470–481. https://doi.org/10.1177/0081246317737916

Brennan, D. (2001). Tourism in transnational places: Dominican sex workers and German sex tourists imagine one another. *Identities, 7*(4), 621–663.

Brents, B. G., Yamashita, T., Spivak, A. L., Venger, O., Parreira, C., & Lanti, A. (2020). Are Men who pay for sex sexist? Masculinity and client attitudes toward gender role equality in different prostitution markets. *Men and Masculinities.* https://doi.org/10.1177/1097184X20901561

Chen, M. H. (2005). Contradictory male sexual desires: Masculinity, lifestyles and sexuality among prostitutes' clients in Taiwan. *Travail, Genre et Societes, 10*, 107–128.

Evans, D. M., Richter, M. L., & Katumba, M. I. (2019). Policing of sex work in South Africa: The positive policing partnership approach. *Journal of Community Safety and Well-Being, 4*(4), 80–85. https://doi.org/10.35502/jcswb.107

Farvid, P., & Braun, V. (2006). "Most of us guys are raring to go anytime, anyplace, anywhere": Male and female sexuality in Cleo and Cosmo. *Sex Roles, 55*, 295–310.

Frank, K. (2003). "Just trying to relax": Masculinity, masculinizing practices, and strip club regulars. *The Journal of Sex Research, 40*(1), 61–75.

Gardner, J. (2009). Criminalising the act of sex: Attitudes to adult commercial sex work in South Africa. In M. Steyn & M. Van Zyl (Eds.), *The price and the prize* (pp. 329–340). HSRC Press.

Garrick, D. (2005). Excuses, excuses: Rationalisations of Western sex tourists in Thailand. *Current Issues in Tourism, 8*(6), 497–509.

Gezinski, L. B., Karandikar, S., Levitt, A., & Ghaffarian, R. (2016). "Total girlfriend experience": Examining marketplace mythologies on sex tourism websites. *Culture, Health & Sexuality, 18*(7), 785–798.

Gilman, S. L. (1985). Black bodies, white bodies: Toward an iconography of female sexuality in late nineteenth-century art, medicine, and literature. *Critical Inquiry, 12*(1), 204–242.

Gould, C. (2014). Sex trafficking and prostitution in South Africa. *The Annals of the American Academy of Political and Social Science, 653*(1), 183–201.

Gould, C., & Fick, N. (2008). *Selling sex in Cape Town: Sex work and human trafficking in a South African city.* Institute for Security Studies.

Hammond, N., & Hooff, J. van. (2019). "This is me, This is what I am, I am a man": The masculinities of men who pay for sex with women. *The Journal of Sex Research,* 1–14. https://doi.org/10.1080/00224499.2019.1644485

Hewer, R. M. (2021). *Sex-work, prostitution and policy: A feminist discourse analysis*. Palgrave Macmillan. https://doi.org/10.1007/978-3-030-74954-5

Hoang, K. (2010). Economies of emotion, familiarity, fantasy, and desire: Emotional labor in Ho Chi Minh city's sex industry. *Sexualities, 13*(2), 255–272.

Hollway, W. (2001). Gender difference and the production of subjectivity. In M. Wetherell, S. Taylor, & S. J. Yates (Eds.), *Discourse theory and practice: A reader* (pp. 272–284). Sage.

Holzman, H. R., & Pines, S. (1982). Buying sex: The phenomenology of being a john. *Deviant Behavior, 4*(1), 89–116.

Huff, A. (2011). Buying the girlfriend experience: An exploration of the consumption experiences of male customers of escorts. *Research in Consumer Behavior, 13*, 111–126.

Huschke, S., & Coetzee, J. (2019). Sex work and condom use in Soweto, South Africa: A call for community-based interventions with clients. *Culture, Health & Sexuality*, 1–15. https://doi.org/10.1080/13691058.2019.1568575

Huschke, S., & Schubotz, D. (2016). Commercial sex, clients, and Christian morals: Paying for sex in Ireland. *Sexualities, 19*(7), 869–887.

Huysamen, M. (2016). Constructing the "respectable" client and the "good" researcher: The complex dynamics of cross-gender interviews with men who pay for sex. *NORMA: International Journal for Masculinity Studies, 11*(1), 19–33.

Huysamen, M. (2017). *A critical analysis of men's constructions of paying for sex: Doing gender, doing race in the interview context* [Doctoral dissertation, University of Cape Town].

Huysamen, M. (2019). Queering the "straight" line: Men's talk on paying for sex. *Journal of Gender Studies, 28*(5), 519–530. https://doi.org/10.1080/09589236.2018.1546570

Huysamen, M. (2020). "There's massive pressure to please her": On the discursive production of men's desire to pay for sex. *The Journal of Sex Research, 57*(5), 639–649. https://doi.org/10.1080/00224499.2019.1645806

Huysamen, M., & Boonzaier, F. (2015). Men's constructions of masculinity and male sexuality through talk of buying sex. *Culture, Health & Sexuality, 17*(5), 541–554.

Huysamen, M., & Boonzaier, F. (2018). "Out of Africa": Racist discourse in men's talk on sex work. *Psychology in Society, 57*, 58–80.

Huysamen, M., & Richter, M. (2020). *Towards harm reduction programmes with sex worker clients in South Africa*. Sonke Gender Justice. https://genderjustice.org.za/download/towards-harm-reduction-programmes-with-sex-worker-clients-in-south-africa/

Jewkes, R., Morrell, R., Sikweyiya, Y., Dunkle, K., & Penn-Kekana, L. (2012a). Men, prostitution and the provider role: Understanding the intersections of economic exchange, sex, crime and violence in South Africa. *PLoS One, 7*(7), e40821.

Jewkes, R., Morrell, R., Sikweyiya, Y., Dunkle, K., & Penn-Kekana, L. (2012b). Transactional relationships and sex with a woman in prostitution:

Prevalence and patterns in a representative sample of South African men. *BMC Public Health, 12*(1), 325.

Joseph, L., & Black, P. (2012). Who's the man? Fragile masculinities, consumer masculinities, and the profiles of sex work clients. *Men and Masculinities, 15*, 486–506.

Karim, Q. A., Karim, S. S., Soldan, K., & Zondi, M. (1995). Reducing the risk of HIV infection among South African sex workers: Socioeconomic and gender barriers. *American Journal of Public Health, 85*, 1521–1525.

Katsulis, Y. (2010). "Living like a king": Conspicuous consumption, virtual communities, and the social construction of paid sexual encounters by U.S. sex tourists. *Men and Masculinities, 13*(2), 210–230.

Kong, T. S. K. (2015). Romancing the boundary: Client masculinities in the Chinese sex industry. *Culture, Health & Sexuality, 17*(7), 810–824.

Lawless, S., Kippax, S., & Crawford, J. (1996). Dirty, diseased and undeserving: The positioning of HIV positive women. *Social Science & Medicine, 43*(9), 1371–1377.

Levine, P. (2003). *Prostitution, race, and politics: Policing venereal disease in the British Empire.* Routledge.

McKeganey, N. (1994). Why do men buy sex and what are their assessments of the HIV-related risks when they do? *AIDS Care, 6*(3), 289–301.

Mgbako, C. (2016). *To live freely in this world: Sex worker activism in Africa.* New York University Press.

Milrod, C., & Monto, M. (2012). The hobbyist and the girlfriend experience: Behaviors and preferences of male customers of internet sexual service providers. *Deviant Behavior, 33*, 792–810.

Monto, M. (2004). Female prostitution, customers, and violence. *Violence Against Women, 10*, 160–188.

Monto, M., & McRee, N. (2005). A comparison of the male customers of female street prostitutes with national samples of men. *International Journal of Offender Therapy and Comparative Criminology, 49*(5), 505–529.

O'Connell Davidson, J. (2000). Sex tourism and child prostitution. In S. Clift & C. Carter (Eds.), *Tourism and sex: Culture, commerce and coercion* (pp. 54–74). Continuum Publishing.

Patton, C. (1990). Inventing "African AIDS". *New Formations, 10*, 25–39.

Pitts, M. K., Smith, A. M. A., Grierson, J., O'Brien, M., & Misson, S. (2004). Who pays for sex and why? An analysis of social and motivational factors associated with male clients of sex workers. *Archives of Sexual Behavior, 33*(4), 353–358.

Platt, L., Grenfell, P., Meiksin, R., Elmes, J., Sherman, S. G., Sanders, T., Mwangi, P., & Crago, A. L. (2018). Associations between sex work laws and sex workers' health: A systematic review and meta-analysis of quantitative and qualitative studies. *PLoS Medicine, 15*(12), e1002680. https://doi.org/10.1371/journal.pmed.1002680

Plumridge, E. W., Chetwynd, S. J., Reed, A. J., & Gifford, S. J. (1997). Discourses of emotionality in commercial sex: The missing client voice. *Feminism & Psychology, 7*(2), 165–181.

Potts, A. (2000a). Coming, coming, gone: A feminist deconstruction of heterosexual orgasm. *Sexualities*, *3*, 55–76.

Potts, A. (2000b). "The essence of the hard on": Hegemonic masculinity and the cultural construction of "erectile dysfunction". *Men and Masculinities*, *3*(1), 85–103.

Prior, A., & Peled, E. (2019). Paying for sex while traveling as tourists: The experiences of Israeli men. *The Journal of Sex Research*, *56*, 659–669. https://doi.org/10.1080/00224499.2018.1530340

Prior, A., & Peled, E. (2021). Identity construction of men who pay women for sex: A qualitative meta-synthesis. *The Journal of Sex Research*. www.tandfonline.com/doi/abs/10.1080/00224499.2021.1905763

Richter, M., & Bodin, C. (2017). Adult, consensual sex work in South Africa – the cautionary message of criminal law and sexual morality. *South African Journal on Human Rights*, *25*(2), 179–197. https://doi.org/10.1080/19962126.2009.11865199

Richter, M., Chersich, M. F., Vearey, J., Sartorius, B., Temmerman, M., & Luchters, S. (2014). Migration status, work conditions and health utilization of female sex workers in three South African cities. *Journal of Immigrant and Minority Health*, *16*(1), 7–17.

Richter, M., Wasserman, Z., & Lakhani, I. (2020). Targets of hate, shame or exploitation?: The (violent) conundrum of sex work in democratic South Africa. *International Journal of Critical Diversity Studies*, *3*(1), 9–24. https://doi.org/10.13169/intecritdivestud.3.1.0009

Sanders, T. (2008). Male sexual scripts: Intimacy, sexuality and pleasure in the purchase of commercial sex. *Sociology*, *42*(3), 400–417.

Sanders, T. (2009). Kerbcrawler rehabilitation programmes: Curing the "deviant" male and reinforcing the "respectable" moral order. *Critical Social Policy*, *29*(1), 77–99. https://doi.org/10.1177/0261018308098395

Sanders, T. (2012). *Paying for pleasure: Men who buy sex*. Routledge.

Sanders, T., Brents, B. G., & Wakefield, C. (2020). *Paying for sex in a digital age: US and UK perspectives*. Routledge.

Sanders, T., & Campbell, R. (2008). Why hate men who pay for sex? Exploring the shift to "tackling demand" in the UK. In V. Munro (Ed.), *Demanding sex? Critical reflections on the supply/demand dynamic in prostitution* (pp. 179–193). Ashgate.

Scorgie, F., Nakato, D., Harper, E., Richter, M., Maseko, S., Nare, P., Smit, J., & Chersich, M. (2013). "We are despised in the hospitals": Sex workers' experiences of accessing health care in four African countries. *Culture, Health & Sexuality*, *15*(4), 450–465. https://doi.org/10.1080/13691058.2012.763187

Smith, M., & Mac, J. (2018). *Revolting prostitutes: The fight for sex workers' rights*. Verso Books.

South African Law Reform Commission. (2017). *Report on sexual offenses: Adult prostitution*. www.justice.gov.za/salrc/reports/r-pr107-SXO-Adult-Prostitution-2017.pdf

Stadler, J., & Delany, S. (2006). The "healthy brothel": The context of clinical services for sex workers in Hillbrow, South Africa. *Culture, Health & Sexuality, 8*(5), 451–464.

Statistics South Africa. (2017). *Poverty trends in South Africa: An examination of absolute poverty between 2006 and 2015.* www.statssa.gov.za/publications/Report-03-10-06/Report-03-10-062015.pdf

Stone, J., Mukandavire, C., Boily, M. C., Fraser, H., Mishra, S., Schwartz, S., Rao, A., Looker, K. J., Quaife, M., Terris-Prestholt, F., Marr, A., Lane, T., Coetzee, J., Gray, G., Otwombe, K., Milovanovic, M., Hausler, H., Young, K., Mcingana, M., . . . Vickerman, P. (2021). Estimating the contribution of key populations towards HIV transmission in South Africa. *Journal of the International AIDS Society, 24*(1), e25650. https://doi.org/10.1002/jia2.25650

Townsend, L., Jewkes, R., Mathews, C., Johnston, L. G., Flisher, A. J., Zembe, Y., & Chopra, M. (2011). HIV risk behaviours and their relationship to intimate partner violence (IPV) among men who have multiple female sexual partners in Cape Town, South Africa. *AIDS and Behavior, 15*(1), 132–141. https://doi.org/10.1007/s10461-010-9680-5

Trotter, H. (2008). *Sugar girls & seamen: A journey into the world of dockside prostitution in South Africa.* Jacana Media.

UNAIDS. (2016). *Prevention gap report.* www.unaids.org/sites/default/files/media_asset/2016-prevention-gap-report_en.pdf

van Brunschot, E. G. (2003). Community policing and "john schools". *Canadian Review of Sociology/Revue Canadienne de Sociologie, 40*(2), 215–232.

Van Heyningen, E. B. (1984). The social evil in the Cape colony 1868–1902: Prostitution and the contagious diseases acts. *Journal of Southern African Studies, 10*(2), 170–197. https://doi.org/10.1080/03057078408708077

Weitzer, R. (2018). Resistance to sex work stigma. *Sexualities, 21*(5–6), 717–729.

Wojcicki, J. M., & Malala, J. (2001). Condom use, power and HIV/AIDS risk: Sex-workers bargain for survival in Hillbrow/Joubert Park/Berea, Johannesburg. *Social Science & Medicine, 53*(1), 99–121.

Xantidis, L., & McCabe, M. P. (2000). Personality characteristics of male clients of female commercial sex workers in Australia. *Archives of Sexual Behavior, 29*(2), 165–176.

Yingwana, N., Walker, D. R., & Etchart, A. (2019). Sex work, migration, and human trafficking in South Africa: From polarised arguments to potential partnerships. *Anti-Trafficking Review, 12*, 74–90. https://doi.org/10.14197/atr.201219125

Zatz, N. D. (1997). Sex work/sex act: Law, labor, and desire in constructions of prostitution. *Signs, 22*(2), 277–308.

Zoia, F. T. P. (2015). *Sanitizing South Africa: Race, racism and germs in the making of the Apartheid state, 1880–1980* [Doctoral dissertation, Indiana University]. http://gradworks.umi.com.ezproxy.uct.ac.za/37/02/3702579.html

2

AN ASSEMBLAGE OF THEORIES, METHODS, AND PRACTICE

Towards a critical reflexive approach

Introduction

This chapter provides a theoretical framing for the critical reflexive approach I present throughout this book. This critical reflexive approach is not a step-by-step research guide. Rather, it is an assemblage of established theoretical and methodological frames and approaches broadly from within poststructuralist and psychoanalytic thought that are used together to build reflexivity into the research design with the intention of deepening the theoretical insights into the topics we study. The current chapter is divided into two parts. The first part introduces the epistemological assumptions of the book and describes the collection of theoretical and philosophical approaches that underpin it. The second provides a critical introduction to the particular research methods, processes, and tools that I used in my study to interview men about paying for sex in South Africa.

Epistemological framework

The ontological and epistemological assumptions underpinning our research inevitably shape the kinds of research questions we ask. Our conceptions of the nature of reality and how it can be known will determine what we want to know about our research topic and how we believe we can come to know it (Willig, 2001). Theory and method should, therefore, be difficult, if not impossible, to extricate from one another. Whether we do so consciously or not, when we narrow down a research

DOI: 10.4324/9781003093602-2

question or choose a method of data collection, we have already made epistemological decisions that will underpin our entire research process.

Given the centrality of epistemology and ontology to the research process, it is apt to start by defining these rather slippery terms.[1] Perhaps the simplest definition of these complex philosophical concepts that I have encountered is, "Ontology = Stuff. Epistemology = About Stuff". Ontology is concerned with the nature of reality (stuff). Epistemology is concerned with how we speak about, perceive, represent, or come to know about reality (stuff). Otherwise put, your ontological position is your view of the world. Your epistemological position is how you think we come to know things and learn things about the world (Kara, 2020). In this book, I focus on the epistemological foundations of the social constructionist approach. That is the "how do we come to know, perceive, represent, understand, and experience stuff?" of the social constructionist approach.

The critical reflexive research approach I describe throughout this book is grounded in a social constructionist epistemology. The first step to understanding what social constructionism is involves being clear about what it is *not*. Social constructionism is not positivism. Research in psychology, like much of the social sciences, functions within an academic context where the positivist research enjoys hegemonic status (Hollway & Jefferson, 2013). Central to positivist epistemology is the assumption of a straightforward and direct relationship between reality and representation (Braun & Clarke, 2013; Willig, 2001). This informs an approach to research that assumes that under the right conditions it is possible for researchers to uncover the "truth" about and represent reality/the world/stuff more or less exactly as it. For the positivist researcher, research data (be that interview data, statistics, experimental results) act as a mirror to reality. Positivist research aims to produce objective knowledge that is impartial or unbiased, using results generated by a researcher who is neutral and has little or no impact on the research process. A social constructionist approach shares none of these assumptions.

Like all hegemonies, positivist epistemological assumptions often become the benchmark against which all ways of doing research are measured – they become *the* way of doing research, rather than just one way of doing research. When our work is placed under the scrutiny of ethics committees, publishers, peer reviewers, and funding bodies who are less familiar with constructionist epistemological positions, they are likely to make demands of our research that are based on positivist epistemological assumptions. However, research conducted within a social constructionist framework does not answer to the assumptions and imperatives of positivist epistemology. When a peer reviewer critiques qualitative research design for its inability to be replicated precisely by another researcher, or questions its relatively smaller sample size or lack of generalisability, it is akin to judging the quality of an apple on its ability to fly. Social constructionism and positivism are based on profoundly different understandings of how the world is known and represented (Hollway & Jefferson, 2013).

Central to the social constructionist approach is the assumption that the meanings we make of the world are socially constituted through language and contextually situated in time and place. Central to this epistemological approach is the focus on the constructive or productive function of language. A constructionist approach does not necessarily assume that all objects ("stuff") are socially constructed and therefore do not exist outside of these constructions, but it does assume that all of our understandings, perceptions, and experiences of these objects ("about stuff") are socially constructed (Edley, 2001). Edley reflects that,

> as soon as we begin to think or talk about the world, we neces-
> sarily begin to represent. Talk involves the creation or construc-
> tion of particular accounts or stories of what the world is like.
>
> *(Edley, 2001, p. 437)*

Rather than the straightforward link between words and the world, "'reality' isn't so much mirrored in talk and texts as it is constituted by them" (Edley, 2001, p. 435). Language and discourse bring objects into being as objects of our understanding and perception. It is in this sense that the world as we *experience* it cannot exist outside of language and representation(s). From this epistemological framework, rather than being concerned with uncovering a single "truth" about the world, researchers understand "truths" about the world to be multiple, ever-changing, and contradictory.

An assemblage of theories

There are an array of theoretical positions and approaches that are grounded in the social constructionist assumption that language is a constructive process. These theories and schools of thought vary in their aims and focus, but they all understand language as constitutive of meaning and subjectivity. The critical reflexive approach that I present in this book is built from an assemblage of these theories.

My approach is particularly influenced by poststructuralist thought. I understand poststructuralism as collection of theoretical positions that are particular variants of social constructionism (Gavey, 2011). Poststructuralism is generally concerned with deconstructing and destabilising existing social categories, such as race, class, gender, sex, and sexuality (Boonzaier, 2006). As Gavey argues, poststructuralist ideas invite "questions that could take us beyond the surface of our culturally shared commonsense understandings of the world" (Gavey, 2011, p. 184). Rather than accepting such categories as natural and essential, poststructuralists unpack these norms, showing how they only have meaning in the historical, social, political, economic, and intellectual contexts within which they exist (Gavey, 2011).

Poststructuralism, along with other constructionist approaches, diverges from mainstream academic psychology in how it views the subjectivity and the self (Gavey, 1989). From a poststructuralist position, language constitutes subjectivity (Gavey, 1989). This calls for the decentring of the subject, shifting focus away from the individual towards the sociocultural contexts and structural conditions that enable the individual accounts we collect in our research (Braun & Clarke, 2006; Wetherell, 2008). Traditionally, psychology focuses heavily on the individual, and assumes that each person has a unified, coherent, and rational self from where unique and authentic individual experiences, motivations, and subjectivities emerge (Gavey, 1989). Poststructuralism rejects the notion that there is a stable and unified subject that can come to be known and understood with certainty. Unlike traditional psychology, it assumes a subject that is contradictory, inconsistent, and fragmented (Gavey, 1989). This is why looking out for inconsistencies and contradictions in our participants' talk is an important part of the critical reflexive approach (Hollway & Jefferson, 2013).

The critical reflexive approach outlined in this book is the product of "careful eclecticism": theoretical picking and choosing, drawing from various theoretical sources – including feminist poststructuralist theory, queer theory, intersectionality theory, critical discourse theory, feminist decolonial theories, as well as psychoanalytic and psychosocial theories – to build this understanding of the research process and the way that knowledge is produced there. This critical reflexive approach does not depend on an exact formulaic amalgamation of these theories.

A spirit of theoretical and methodological eclecticism, an invitation to draw on complimentary theoretical approaches, underpins this critical reflexive approach. Next, I outline these theories that together make up the critical reflexive approach I used in this study.

Feminist poststructuralism

Feminist poststructuralism is a branch of poststructuralism with a feminist agenda and central focus on understanding gender as socially constructed rather than biologically determined (Gavey, 1989; Weedon, 1987). Feminist poststructuralist theory is particularly useful for understanding research around sexual topics because of its explicit focus on gender (Gavey, 1989, 2011). Two of the central aims or interests of feminist poststructuralism are acknowledging the existing gendered power relations of everyday life and identifying areas and opportunities for resistance or change (Weedon, 1987). As Gavey (1989) states, "rather than 'discovering' reality, 'revealing' truth or 'uncovering' the facts, feminist poststructuralism would, instead, be concerned with disrupting and displacing dominant (oppressive) knowledges" (p. 436).

Discursive approaches

The term "discourse" as I use it here is not limited only to language or text, but any signs, symbols, and other signifying practices that people use to represent themselves to one other (Parker, 2004). Discourses can be defined as different systems of meaning for understanding, experiencing, and acting in the world (Parker, 2004). Discourses stipulate how ideas about a particular issue (e.g. sex work, fatherhood, or femininity) are put into practice and establish rules that restrict and punish alternative ways of knowing, talking about, or conducting ourselves in relation to these issues within a particular socio-historical context (Parker, 1992, 2004). How people come to talk about, make meaning of, and perceive any experience is filtered through the discourses that are available in that particular time and context. For example, Butler argues that the body itself is not only material or biological but also represents a "set of historic possibilities" (1988, p. 521); what these possibilities for the body might be (in other words, what we can do with our bodies) are constrained or made conceivable by the discourses available at any given time and place. Discourses vary in the level of authority that they wield. Dominant discourses are often so entrenched that they are viewed as natural: they invoke appeals to common-sense understandings of the world and are accepted as being the natural order of things, or just "the way things are" rather than as particular versions of knowledge (Gavey, 1989; Willig, 2001).

Discourses construct and make available an array of subject positions for individuals to take up; we are positioned within and by the discourse (Hall, 2001). As Weedon (1987, p. 119) contends, "to speak is to assume a subject position within discourse and to become subjected to the power and regulation of the discourse". Discourse and power are always relational (Foucault, 1981; Weedon, 1987). These subject positions are always taken up in relation to others.

A discursive approach brings to the forefront the relationship between power and knowledge (Henriques et al., 2002). Foucault (1981) suggests that power relations are not a simple unidirectional relationship between the powerful and the powerless. Instead, these relationships of power are more complicated, intricate, often contradictory, and are organised differently in different societies through relations of race, class, gender, religion, or age (Weedon, 1987). Power and discourse are mutually constitutive; power is not only an effect of discourse, but also discourse is an effect of power (Henriques et al., 2002). Weedon highlights the multiplicity of power relations specifically focused on sexuality and warns that a failure to understand or acknowledge this multiplicity in a feminist analysis will render the analysis incapable of identifying the potential points of resistance. Foucault (1981, p. 124) poignantly argues that, "sexuality is an especially dense transfer point for relations of power: between men and women, young people and old people, parents and offspring, teachers and students, priests and laity, an administration and a population". Given the assumption that sexuality is a primary locus of power, this book – which explores constructions of gender, sexuality, and race in a context where a woman interviews men about paying for sex in South Africa – represents an important site for the analysis of this complex notion of power.

Performance, performativity, and queer theory

In developing the critical reflexive approach that I employ in this book, I have found the concept of "doing" gender (West & Zimmerman, 1987), the assumption that gender is something that is performed, a useful starting point. The notion of "doing gender" implies that by constantly performing everyday acts commonly associated with, or expected of, a particular gender within a particular society, we become intelligible as being of that gender (Pini, 2005). Queer theorists such as Judith Butler (1999, 2008) and Sara Ahmed (2006) build on this by providing a less unidirectional approach to gender – they theorise gender not only as performed but also as *performative*. Butler posits that it is not purely because we are assigned "male" or "female" genders at birth, or identify as a man or a woman, that we perform certain corresponding gendered acts, but that through repeatedly performing these seemingly mundane acts, we *become* gendered. In this sense, the gendered subject is also created through their actions, rather than these actions merely proceeding from a stable gendered identity. At the heart of Butler's theory of performativity are the notions of repetition, citation, and mimicking (Butler, 1999, 2008). Butler challenges the rigid dichotomies of gender by defining gender as "a stylized repetition of acts" (Butler, 1988, p. 519). She suggests that it is through the repetition of certain acts, which take place within highly gendered, rigid regulatory schemas, that we become gendered. Over time, the repetition of these acts produces the illusion of a coherent, natural, "normal", or biologically gendered way of being (Butler, 2004).

Ahmed's (2006, 2007) work on *orientation*, and her focus on bodies and spatiality, are also central to the present book. Ahmed's theorising is useful for informing an intersectional approach, as it attends directly to questions of race. Ahmed is also interested in repetition and habit, arguing that our bodies get directed, they "become" as a result of the repetition of certain acts over time: "what bodies 'tend to do' are effects of histories rather than being ordinary" (Ahmed, 2006, p. 56). Just like a skill that becomes effortless through working hard at it, it is through repeating certain gendered and racialised acts, occupying some spaces and not others, and keeping a close proximity to certain bodies and not others, that these categories become naturalised and thus invisible (Ahmed, 2006).

Intersectionality and feminist decolonial theories

The term *intersectionality* was first coined by Kimberle Crenshaw to articulate the complexity of oppressions faced by black women in the Global North (Crenshaw, 1991). It critiques the assumption that all women are affected in the same way by gender stratification, an assumption that works to silence the multiple oppressions that black and other marginalised women face (McCall, 2005). Intersectionality theory suggests that people's gendered identities will always be intersected by their other social identities, such as race, class, sexuality, religion, (dis)ability, and age, in dynamic and complex ways. These various social categories cannot be understood as separate from one another. Rather, these interlocking systems of oppressions (such as race, class, and gender) are seen to be mutually constitutive and work together to maintain the oppression of some and the dominance of others (Collins, 1990; Crenshaw, 1991).

To facilitate a deeper understanding of how structures of oppression may operate in relation to gender and sexuality, I draw on feminist decolonial theory (Boonzaier, 2017; Boonzaier et al., 2020; Lugones, 2010). Feminist decolonial theory goes beyond interpreting various categories or vectors of power as intersecting and argues for an understanding of these structures as fused and indiscernible from one another (Lugones, 2007). For example, from a feminist decolonial perspective, gender is always already racialised and racism and neoliberalism are always already gendered (Gill, 2008; Rutherford, 2018).

The psychosocial approach

In addition to poststructuralist theories, I draw psychoanalytic theories and methods to build reflexivity into my research design. Particularly, a key theoretical influence on my understanding of the interview encounter is Hollway and Jefferson's psychosocial approach to the research process. Hollway and Jefferson describe their psychosocial approach as "deeply indebted to psychoanalysis, theoretically and methodologically" (Hollway & Jefferson, 2013, p. 72). While I do not take up every aspect of the psychosocial approach, I draw on Hollway and Jefferson's theory of the defended subject and I use psychoanalytic concepts like "transference" and "counter transference" in a basic way to inform the way I do reflexive research. Unlike a purely discursive approach, Hollway and Jefferson theorise a subject that is not only positioned within available social discourses but also "motivated by unconscious investments and defences against anxiety" (Hollway & Jefferson, 2013, p. 72). They suggest that in every social encounter, people experience anxiety resulting from perceived threats to their identities. The theory of the *defended subject* assumes that people draw on particular available discourses and discursive positions rather than others as defences against these feelings of anxiety. While this approach requires the researcher to deploy the concept of anxiety at the level of individuals, it does not assume that anxiety itself is wholly individual, but rather that it is socially constituted (Hollway & Jefferson, 2013; Hook, 2008). This approach allows the researcher to attend directly to the anxiety associated with threats to identity and its impact on the interview encounter. This is particularly valuable for research about sexual, secretive, or stigmatised sexual practices and desires around which people feel shame and anxiety (Foucault, 1981).

Theorising the interview encounter

Collectively, these theoretical understandings of language, identity, power, gender, and race have implications for how we as researchers understand our research encounters. They have implications for how we understand our participants' narratives and our own position in the research process. As Hollway and Jefferson write, "what do you, the researcher, assume about a person's capacity to know, remember, and tell about themselves?" (Hollway & Jefferson, 2013, p. 150). To answer this, I look to Gavey (1989, p. 466) who suggests that we "should approach the reports and accounts of those we research as discursive productions and not as reflections (accurate, distorted, or otherwise) of their 'true' experience". Indeed, from a social constructionist epistemological framework, the researcher would be less concerned with the accuracy with which experiences are relayed by a particular text or narrative than with the discourses that are drawn upon when they are described.

This has been particularly relevant to my research with men who pay for sex. Some of the questions people often ask me when they hear that I have interviewed men about paying for sex are, "but how do you know the men are telling the truth?" or "how do you know they aren't just making things up to make themselves look like good guys?" I usually reply, "I'm actually quite interested in what kinds of stories men think would make them look like good guys" (see Huysamen, 2016). As Plummer writes (1995, p. 5), instead of viewing sexual stories as "providing rays of real truth on sexual lives – sexual stories can be seen as issues to be investigated in their own right. They become topics to investigate, not merely resources to draw upon". I do not read men's narratives about paying for sex as mirrors of reality that offer factual accounts of what it is really like to pay for sex, or what they are really like as clients, fathers, or husbands. I am interested in which discourses participants draw on and which versions of gender, sexuality, and race they perform in interviews. I am concerned with questions about how participants negotiate their identities and make sense of their lives, in relation to paying for sex, using the discourses available to them.

The critical reflexive approach employed in this book understands both the interviewer and participants as *defended subjects* whose perceptions of each other are not purely derived from a "real" research relationship but are influenced by their own histories and relationships and the personal anxieties that they bring into the research relationship (Hollway & Jefferson, 2013). Therefore, the interviewer and the participant both can be understood as defended subjects who deploy certain discourses and distance themselves from others to defend against these anxieties in the moment of the interview. Rather than simply being concerned with *what* people say in interviews, this approach attends to "the complex social process involved in the tellings" (Plummer, 1995, p. 13).

Central to a critical reflexive approach is applying to the research context the idea of gender as performed and *performative*. If we accept that we are all gendered subjects and that we are all constantly "doing" gender as we go about our daily lives, then we must accept that our research interviews would in no way be immune to this "doing" of gender. Weedon (1987, p. 87) suggests that, "in patriarchal societies we cannot escape the implications of femininity. Everything we do signifies compliance or resistance to dominant norms of what it is to be a woman". In our interviews, we as researchers, as well as our participants, must constantly be doing gender in relation to one another. Drawing on intersectionality and feminist decolonial theory, if we are constantly doing gender and sexuality in the research context, we must simultaneously be doing all our other intersecting and fused social identities, like race and class. I extend Weedon's theorising to suggest that we also cannot escape the implications of colonialism and coloniality; everything we do signifies compliance or resistance to these systems of oppression. Consequently, interviews become sites where subjectivities and subjects are not only explored but also they are actually *produced* (Sandberg, 2011). They become not only contexts where participants' narrative accounts are collected but also sites within which both the participant *and* the researcher perform, negotiate, resist, and construct their identities in relation to one another. Therefore, all the interactions between the participant and researcher in the interview encounter become part of the data.

To theorise the interview context in this way – as a place where the researcher's and participant's intersecting identities are performed, produced, and defended – is to acknowledge the impossibility of neutrality and objectivity within the research process. It is to acknowledge that meaning is co-constructed by the researcher and the participant. It is to accept that the researcher is implicated in every stage of the research process, and that their presence has the potential to both facilitate and limit what can be said in their interviews (Hollway & Jefferson, 2013). As Plummer reflects, "the social scientist is part of the very process of being observed, analysed, and ultimately written about: I am part of this process and it is deeply social" (Plummer, 1995, p. 12). Such an approach not only contests the assumptions of researcher's neutrality, objectivity, and detachedness prized by positivist research approaches but also embraces the complexity of the research process and celebrates researchers' acknowledgement and analysis of it (Huysamen, 2020).

Reflexivity

This book presents an approach to the research process that puts a great deal of weight on reflexivity. It differs from the kind of reflexivity that is commonly advocated in more traditional qualitative research processes (yet seldom expected of quantitative researchers), where the researcher, in a paragraph in the methods section, might append a few generic lines acknowledging that their race, class, and gender might impact the research process. In feminist research, it is regarded as common practice for the researcher to acknowledge their positionality within the research and to reflexively explore how their research is produced. Reflexivity has been widely engaged by feminist researchers because it is epistemologically and ontologically connected with the feminist critique of knowledge and knowledge production (Pini, 2004). Like other critical feminist scholars who have explored the dilemmas and dynamics of interviewing in the field of masculinities (e.g. Arendell, 1997; Boonzaier, 2017; Broom et al., 2009; Gadd, 2004; Gottzén, 2013; Grenz, 2005; Presser, 2005; Sandberg, 2011; Winchester, 1996), I place interviewer–participant dynamics at the centre of my research focus. These dynamics then become part of my data. Such an approach to reflexivity involves employing an analysis of the researcher's subjectivity and its impact on the research process to actively facilitate the analytical process (Hollway & Jefferson, 2013).

This type of reflexivity is not secondary to the main analysis, but, as will be demonstrated in each chapter of this book, built into the very design of the research process.

An eclectic approach to data analysis

As may be clear by now, a "careful eclecticism" is central to the critical reflexive approach, and this also applies to the process of data analysis. I draw on different theoretical and methodological approaches to aid my analytical process. I think of these approaches as lenses, the kind you might encounter when going for an eye test, each one sliding on top of the other, slightly sharpening or altering my focus, adding a different shade, and changing the way I see, attend to, and interpret my interview data. These are the combination of (more or less) compatible approaches that work for and with the data. They are a collection of approaches that I have found and that have found me along my research journey. They are not a magic combination. You may choose to assemble your analytical frame slightly differently but have similar goals and underlying understandings of the research process and still call it a critical reflexive approach akin to mine. Next, I outline some of the analytic approaches that I used in analysing the data presented in this book.

Discourse analysis

Discourse analysis is not one coherent, unified approach to analysing data. The term means different things to different people. Discourse analysis refers broadly to a set of methods that employ different theories of language with the aim of identifying discursive patterns of meaning as well as inconsistencies and contradictions in a text (Gavey, 1989). Like Gavey (1989), I see it as a process of naming the language people use to constitute their own and other's identities.

I draw on two different analytic frameworks for discourse analysis. The first is critical or *Foucauldian discourse analysis* (Parker, 1992, 2004), much of which I have already delineated in the previous section of this chapter. At its core, this approach examines how language is deployed to construct particular objects and subjects, and how these are relational and invested with power (Boonzaier, 2017). The second approach, often referred to as *discursive psychology*, is inspired by conversation analysis and ethnomethodology (Wetherell, 1998). Here, the interest lies in *how* people use the discursive resources available to them to negotiate certain identities and achieve certain interpersonal aims within their immediate social interactions such as in interviews. It is the "talk-in-action", as Wetherell (Wetherell, 1998, p. 395) terms it, that is of interest. In other words, this approach to discourse analysis is interested in what people "do" or accomplish with language and places emphasis on the performative nature of discourse (Wetherell, 1998; Willig, 2001). Inspired by conversation analysis, this approach is more interested in the immediate social context within which the language occurs. One might imagine Foucauldian analysis as zooming out to see the broader social structures and discursive psychology as zooming in to understand how these broader discourses and meanings are used and operate within individual social encounters. Data analysis from this perspective would pay careful attention to even the smallest inter-action between the interviewer and participant, noting features such as pauses, turn-taking, intonations, and repetitions, and analysing how their responses to one another may serve to do things for their identity and achieve interpersonal objectives (Wetherell, 1998; Willig, 2001).

In psychology, it has been common to differentiate between the two kinds of discourse analysis, despite the clear overlap that exists between these approaches (Wetherell, 1998; Willig, 2001). However, Wetherell (1998, p. 402) argues for a more integrated, eclectic approach which draws on both schools of thought: "if the problem with post-structuralist analysts is that they rarely focus on actual social interaction, then the problem with conversational analysts is that they rarely raise their eyes from the next turn in the conversation". Taking heed on this critique, I relied on an eclectic approach to analysing discursive patterns within the data. Drawing on the Foucauldian approach, I identified the various available discourses of, for example, gender, sexuality, race, class, and sex work that participants drew upon. But, due to my interest in how meaning was co-constructed within the interview, I also attended to the immediate interview context. I explored how these discourses were deployed in the moment of the interview to achieve certain interpersonal objectives, for instance, to justify behaviour, to make a participant feel comfortable, or to establish or contest the other person's position of power in the interview. I identified the subject positions that these discourses offered participants and myself in the moment of the interview and explored the relative object positions that were constructed as a result. I questioned what implications these subject positions had for participants' ability to negotiate their identities and relative positions of power, both in the interviewer–participant context and in talking about and making sense of their lives more broadly. I also identified paradoxes and contradictions in the discourses that participants and I drew upon. I looked at the ways in which these discourses, employed by participants and myself, reproduced existing gender relations, as well as moments where they somehow offered possibilities for resistance or change (Gavey, 1989).

Narrative analysis

Central to this critical reflexive approach is attending carefully to the stories that people tell. Narrative theory emerges from the constructionist paradigm, but what sets narrative analysis apart from the discursive approaches to data analysis outlined earlier is its focus on the stories that people tell. Here, we again adjust focus to whole stories within the data. From a narrative perspective, the researcher is not only concerned with identifying the discourses that are embedded in the stories that participants tell, but also with how these discourses are communicated, conveyed, and performed *through* these stories. Thus, keeping these stories whole, rather than fragmenting them during the analysis process, is key to this approach (Riessman, 2008).

Personal narratives make for interesting units of analysis because they are not merely neutral and passive accounts of events. Instead, stories are "social actions embedded in social worlds" (Plummer, 1995, p. 17). They are strategic and functional; in other words, narratives *do* things (Riessman, 2002). Riessman suggests that narratives may be used by individuals to "remember, argue, justify, persuade, engage, entertain, and even mislead" their audience (Riessman, 2008, p. 8) and Plummer reminds us of how stories perform political tasks (Plummer, 1995).

One of the functions of personal narratives is the construction of selfhood and identity. According to narrative theory, it is through narratives that we create ourselves (Crossley, 2000). When an individual tells a story about their life, they are performing a *preferred* version of their identity which they wish to convey to the *specific* audience (Riessman, 2002, 2008). Therefore, exploring what the narrative unit under analysis "does" or accomplishes is a core aim of the narrative analyst. The researcher focuses on which stories participants choose to convey, how they portray these stories, and the identities that they consequently construct through telling these stories.

In this research, participants arrived to tell their sexual stories. Ken Plummer, in his book *Telling Sexual Stories*, defines sexual stories as "simply narratives of the intimate life, focused especially around the erotic, the gendered and the relational" (1995, p. 6). But sexual stories are not necessarily special or separate from other aspects of people's lives. Sexual stories are personal narratives that are "socially embedded in the daily practices of everyday life" (Plummer, 1995, p. 15) and are thus intersected with various other aspects of people's lives and identities.

It is the practice of keeping participant's stories whole, and exploring how identity is performed through these stories, that directly informs the data analysis process that I set out in this book. This approach to participants' narratives can be linked to the concept of *Gestalt*, the understanding that the whole is more than, or different to, the sum of its parts. Hollway and Jefferson (2013) have interpreted and adapted the concept of *Gestalt* to provide practical techniques that researchers can apply to their interviewing to elicit whole narratives, or the interview's *Gestalt*. However, it is also important to reflect on the impossibility of keeping narratives whole, particularly when analysing data and presenting research findings in traditional ways, such as writing up a journal article or a book chapter. Although we prioritise our participants' stories, to say that we as researchers keep our participants' stories whole is to silence the ways in which we inevitably fragment their narratives through our research. Of course, we literally fragment our participants' narratives by only quoting small sections of their talk in the discussion of our findings because of the word and page limits traditional academic mediums place upon us. However, as researchers, we also select which stories to focus on in our analysis and which stories to discard. We decide which parts of our participants' talk constitute a whole story, and in doing so we inevitably isolate smaller stories from larger master narratives, sometimes without recognising this. So, although prioritising participants' narratives in our analysis, and understanding participants' stories as mechanisms for constructing and negotiating their identities is a priority, it is important to also acknowledge the near impossibility of keeping our participants' narratives whole in research.

The research process: interviewing men about paying for sex

In this section, I describe the research process and the methods I employed in this study with 47 men who pay for sex in South Africa. Within the critical reflexive approach there is an imperative to understand research design as a set of research decisions and to think critically about the implications that of each of these decisions will have on your research and the meanings your research will produce as a result. While the methods I have used do not represent a blueprint for doing research according to this approach, the ways in which I think critically about the implications of the research design certainly are.

Research aims

This project's aims were twofold. First, to make a methodological contribution to the fields of qualitative psychology and sex research by employing an approach to sex research that would foreground and interrogate the complex interviewer–participant dynamics operating in the interview and the role they played in shaping the data produced there. Second, the study aimed to contribute to the body of academic knowledge on sex work by exploring how men make meaning of paying for sex in South Africa and how they negotiate their various intersecting identities in relation to this stigmatised practice.

The researcher

The study was conducted by myself, a white middle-class able-bodied cisgender heterosexual woman from Cape Town, South Africa, in my late twenties at the time. The study formed the basis of my doctoral research at the University of Cape Town.

Recruiting participants

Participants were recruited online. I posted advertisements on two online classified websites, Locanto.com and Gumtree.co.za. The call for participants stated that I was a PhD student from the University of Cape Town looking to interview "men who have paid women sex workers for sex" about their experiences and opinions on the topic. I provided an email address where those who were interested in the project could contact me. I offered no compensation for participation, and thus all participants were self-selected and did so voluntarily.

The participants

Forty-three South African men from urban centres across South Africa arrived to tell me about their experiences of paying women for sex. The participants were between the ages of 22 and 67, with a mean age of just over 41. Anyone who identified as a man having paid a woman sex worker for sex (they were free to define and interpret these gender categories as they wished) was eligible to participate. All participants identified as cisgender and they all said that had paid cisgender women for sex. Most participants defined themselves as financially well-established or "comfortable", and most described professional careers (such as engineers, businessmen, or IT specialists) that would place them within middle-class income brackets. Some participants explicitly stated that they were rich or affluent. Most participants were in long-term heterosexual relationships. Specifically, 21 participants said they were in heterosexual marriages, 8 said they were in serious heterosexual relationships, 4 were divorcees from heterosexual marriages, and 10 were single.

I asked each participant to describe how they identified in terms of race or ethnicity. Twenty-six participants identified as white, 13 as Indian, 3 as black, and 1 participant identified as "coloured". Although the classification and segregation of "population groups" has its roots in the colonial period, it was during apartheid that state policies and legislation institutionalised racial discrimination through systematic and deliberate segregation. Under the Population Registration Act (Act No. 30 of 1950), South African citizens were classified into racial categories, "white", "black African", "coloured", "other", and later "Asian" was added. Using categories such as "coloured" in our research is problematic in how it reproduces racist, colonial constructions; this is an issue that many critical scholars working in South Africa grapple with (see e.g. Thumbran, 2019). However, these terms have continuing relevance in South Africa today. I use them because they were the terms that participants used to speak about themselves. Today, the Indian identity refers to South Africans who identify as being of Indian descent (see Landy et al., 2004). However, South African Indian identity is not homogenous, and South African Indians are diverse in origins, language, religious and customary practices, and family values. The South African term "coloured" refers to the diverse group of individuals argued to hold their origins in a range of ethnic groups, including Cape slaves, the indigenous Khoisan population, and other people of African and Asian descent (see van Niekerk, 2019).

Theorising participants as arrivals

Sandberg (2011), in her research with older men theorises research participants as "arrivals":

> The people participating in a study are often referred to as a "sample", a group carefully picked to respond to the needs of

the researcher, often imagined to be representative of a particular social stratum or group. A more appropriate term for the men in this study would, however, be arrivals; more than me choosing them, they chose me, and arrived in this study for various reasons.

(Sandberg, 2011, p. 70)

Rather than taking their participation for granted, understanding our participants as arrivals leads us to ask why our participants decided to arrive to our research in the first place. Chapter 3 is dedicated to exploring this question. Theorising our participants in this way also raises questions around who *did not* arrive for our research, and the implications that these "non-arrivals" have for our interviews and ultimately for our research findings.

Given that paying for sex is both stigmatised and illegal in South Africa, my online recruitment strategy proved to be effective in reaching what is usually considered a "hard-to-reach" group. It also allowed participants from across South Africa to participate in the research. However, my online recruitment strategy predominately attracted middle-class men who were computer literate and had regular access to the Internet, many of whom used the Internet to facilitate their paid sexual activities. Many of these participants enjoyed multiple intersecting privileges. How these intersecting positions of power and privilege played out within the interview, and how this impacted on the kinds of narratives collected, will form a central point of analysis throughout this book.

My online recruitment strategy potentially excluded, and therefore silenced, the voices of poor men who did not have regular access to the Internet and the necessary technologies. In South Africa, where class is still stratified largely along racial lines, this means that many poor black men would have been excluded from the research (Huysamen, 2020). Our qualitative research will almost always be more appealing and/or accessible to some people, and less accessible to others. While we might not have the capacity to control for this in its entirety, it is important that we do reflect on our participants as arrivals, interrogate the conditions under which they have arrived, and be mindful of and explicit about who has not arrived for our research and why.

That the majority of participants were middle-class cisgender white men is not necessarily a shortcoming in this particular study about men who pay for sex in South Africa. As critical reflexive researchers, we must ask questions about what our research, including our methodology, "does" at both the material and discursive levels. Poor, black, and marginalised people tend to be overrepresented in research on stigmatised issues and social problems in South Africa (Huysamen, 2016). When researchers exclusively draw research samples from poor and marginalised groups for their studies on stigmatised social issues like HIV, sex work, or violence, it associates these groups with these issues and gives the impression that they are the only types of people to be affected by these issues, perpetuating existing racist and colonial discourses. For example, Spronk (2014), in their work with black men in Kenya, shows how poor black men in particular have borne the brunt of negative representations in work on masculinity and violence. Spronk (2014) shows how international scholarship on men and masculinities (re)produces the discourse of the hypersexualised black man. Therefore, although it is important to acknowledge the voices that are potentially silenced the research, in the case of this study, researching "privilege" and presenting a critical take on male middle-class heterosexuality in the context of a stigmatised issue such as paying for sex also presented opportunities for resistance.

Interviews

The data in this study were collected through semi-structured narrative interviews. I aimed to provide participants with as many options for participating in these interviews as possible, as the more options we provide our participants for participating in our research, the more accessible and inclusive our research becomes. Those who agreed to participate in the interviews could choose whether they wanted to conduct interviews face-to-face, over the phone, via online video or audio calls, or via online instant messenger (IM) platforms like WhatsApp.

I conducted face-to-face interviews with 11 participants in Cape Town. Face-to-face interviews took place in cafes in areas that suited the participants. The duration of each interview was roughly between 1.5 and 3 hours. Narrative interviews aim to invite participants to tell stories, to elicit long sections of talk, and for participants to guide the interview process as far as possible (Riessman, 2008). I aimed for interviews to be largely unstructured, allowing the participants to lead the interview and determine its pace, tone, and content. However, in reality, the interviews varied along a continuum, from being relatively unstructured to being semi-structured depending on the ease with which individual participants conversed.

I began each interview by asking participants to tell me about themselves in as much or little detail as they felt comfortable as a way of inviting their narratives. From thereon, for those who were comfortable to talk, I allowed them to lead the interviews. I steered the interviews by picking up on certain issues, and asking participants to elaborate on, or provide examples of, the issues that they raised that I was particularly interested in. For those who were not as forthcoming, I had prepared key question areas that would invite participants to tell stories about their experiences. These questions included:

- Tell me about the events leading up to the first time you paid for sex.
- Tell me about a particularly memorable experience of paying for sex.
- How is paid sex different to other kinds of sex you have had?
- Tell me about your experience of the client–sex worker relationship? Are there any boundaries or rules from either side? Who do you think has the most power in the relationship?
- Did you learn anything about yourself or about sex through paying for sex?
- Do/did you have a partner at the time of paying for sex? Do/did they know about your paying for sex?

In an effort to invite participants to reflect on their experience of the interview process, I asked:

- What made you decide to participate in this research?
- How did you find the experience of doing this interview?

All participants were given the option of participating in multiple interviews, although the majority chose to do just one interview. Conducting these interviews in public spaces meant that I did not have to consider the issues relating to my safety that I would have had to consider if I had interviewed participants as a lone researcher in other locations such as their homes. Because of the stigmatised and illegal status of sex work in South Africa, I also had to carefully consider the venues that I selected in relation to issues of anonymity. If I were to have conducted interviews in an interview room at my university, it would have been likely that colleagues, who were aware of my research topic, might have seen my participants coming and going from the interview venue, which could have implicated participants in the illegal and stigmatised activity of paying for sex.

When arranging the interviews in cafes, some participants voiced concerns about privacy and worried that other people might overhear them. However, in practice these environments provided a very easy space to talk about "personal" or "intimate" topics. I selected busy cafes, allowing participants and I to chat freely and casually (like everyone else in the cafe) without anyone realising that we were doing a research interview. This relaxed café setting provided a context that was less threatening and more conducive to having (possibly) difficult conversations than a private office at my university would have been. (On a practical note, be sure not to sit too close to the coffee grinder, these can be disastrous for audio recordings, I have learned.) Conducting interviews in cafes also provided a valuable context to explore my research interest around the "doing" of masculinity and femininity within the interview context. Conducting the interviews in coffee shops not only meant that the participant and I just looked to others like a man and a woman having coffee, but that, to some degree, we also became just a man and woman having coffee. This provided interesting insights into how both the participants and I performed and negotiated masculinity and femininity in the interviews, and the complex ways in which this intersected the researcher–participant dynamics.

Participants were also given the option of doing the interviews either via video calling platforms like Skype or via an instant messaging (IM) chat platform like WhatsApp. I included a recent passport-style photograph as my profile picture on each of the messenger platforms, thus providing participants with a basic idea of who I was in terms of my gender, race, and age.

While the video calls took on much the same pace and format as the face-to-face interviews, the online IM interviews differed in various ways. Participants and I communicated in real time using text messages in a conversational manner (see O'Connor & Madge, 2016 for more on synchronous online interviews). I used the same set of probing questions as I did in face-to-face interviews. However, IM interviews tended to be more structured than the face-to-face and video call interviews. Participants and I also tended to converse in shorter sentences, often using the simple or shortened vernacular that is characteristic of text messaging. Conducting the online IM interviews tended to be a slow process, interviews were generally broken up over several sessions and over a number of days or weeks. In essence, multiple follow-up interviews were conducted with most IM participants.

In general, IM interviews tended to yield answers that were shorter, more to the point, and were very interesting at a content level but perhaps less rich in detail. It was, in most cases, more difficult (but not impossible) to explore the subtler, taken-for-granted performances of gender, race, and class that occurred in the interview in the same way that I could with the face-to-face data. Participants and I also had more time to think about and moderate our answers and questions before responding. Consequently, it is arguable that less was "given away" in the way it often is in face-to-face interviews, where one may, for instance, begin a sentence one way and then correct oneself to sound more socially acceptable.

However, online IM interviews invited a level of disclosure that face-to-face interviews seldom did. For example, three online IM participants told me about their experiences of child sexual abuse, whereas none of my face-to-face participants disclosed anything of that nature. I also collected far more narratives that fell outside of normative heterosexual desire than I did in face-to-face interviews. Perhaps because the IM interviews were time consuming, and the interview relationship was cultivated over a longer period, they allowed for trust and rapport to be established between myself and the participants. Conversely, it could be argued that less trust and rapport is needed online, and that, because of the relative anonymity that the online text platforms provided, participants found it easier to disclose these kinds of details online than they would have if they had been sitting with me face-to-face. Both face-to-face and online IM methods of data collection brought with them their own unique sets of advantages and limitations. Utilising the approaches together afforded the opportunity to collect vast, interesting, and diverse data.

Transcription

Audio recordings were made of the face-to-face and online video call interviews and transcribed verbatim. Because the interviewer–participant interactions and dynamics occurring in the interview are central to the analysis in this critical reflexive approach, when transcribing the face-to-face interview data, I carefully noted the subtle interpersonal communications, such as pauses, body language, sighs, laughter, repetitions, and interruptions. These aspects of the interview form part of the data.

Although the IM interviews were time consuming to conduct, they came with the benefit of being self-transcribing (Kazmer & Xie, 2008). The texts from the online instant messenger interviews were directly transferred into word processor documents that then functioned as the interview transcripts.[2] Participants also automatically had copies of the interviews, which meant that they could read over them again before the next interview if they so wished. In online IM interviews, there were less noticeable micro-communications, such as sighs, pauses, or body language, making the data less rich in this regard. However, because the interviews could be copied and pasted directly from the messenger application, they remained as they were during the interview, meaning that none of the data were changed or lost in the transcription process, making these transcripts particularly valuable in this regard.

Research journal

The research journal is crucial to building critical reflexivity into the research design and an essential part of a critical reflexive approach. I treat the information and details captured in research journals, like reflections about non-verbal communications and emotions, as theoretically and methodologically illuminating. They are a crucial help to researchers as we interpret our data. As you will learn in the chapters that follow, my own anxieties and feelings of excitement, desire, or shame were all directly relevant to the research process. Reflections on interactions like a participant insisting on paying the bill are usually quickly forgotten and then lost at the point of transcription. But within this critical reflexive approach they are captured in research journals and form a key part of the data.

I kept a written research journal throughout the research process. As soon as possible after each interview, I wrote down my reflections of that interview. I noted any observations that I had made and any non-verbal behaviours and interactions that stood out for me. I was careful to note and reflect upon any contradictions or inconsistencies in what participants or I had said or done and made notes about any parts of the interview that puzzled me or did just not quite add up. I have found that these moments often signal rich data and complex issues in the data that require further interrogation.

The critical reflexive approach assumes that the researcher's responses are part of the research data. Our research journals thus become both a research tool to support our analysis and part of the research data. In addition to my immediate post-interview reflections, I noted my own feelings, thoughts, anxieties, frustrations, defences, and other responses that came up during and in the days, weeks, and months after the interview. As the forthcoming chapters will demonstrate, the research journal provided a tool that allowed me to interrogate how my intersecting identities, my defences, and my desires influenced the research process and shaped the data that were co-produced there. It also provided me with rich theoretical insights into participants' subjectivities and their patterns of relating, more so than simply asking them questions would have done. Throughout this book, I will present excerpts from my research journal, which will give you a better understanding of how the research journal is used to aid the critical reflexive research process.

Analysing data

Social constructionist approaches require the researcher to go beyond just organising and describing the data to *interpreting* the data. I began this chapter by describing the assemblage of theoretical approaches (such Foucauldian discourse analysis, discursive psychology, and narrative analysis) that together formed the lens through which I looked to *interpret* the interview data. But I have not yet described the nuts and bolts of how I went about organising and analysing my data. The critical reflexive approach I use does not imply a specific data analysis approach. However, it requires that a careful and systematic scrutiny of the interviewer–participant dynamics be built into the analysis. It assumes that detailed interview transcripts that capture what was said in interviews as well as non-verbal cues will be analysed alongside reflexive journal entries, which are at once part of, and assist with interpreting, the data.

In this study, I analysed (and organised) the data thematically. Broadly, this involves searching for themes and meanings across the data set – in the case of this study, across different participants' narratives. For researchers who like structured data analytic approaches, there are a number (see Attride-Stirling, 2001; Braun & Clarke, 2006), of which perhaps the most popular is the Thematic Analysis (TA) approach outlined by Braun and Clarke (2006). This six-stage process for organising, describing, and interpreting qualitative data is as follows: 1. Data familiarisation; 2. Initial code generation; 3. Identifying and mapping themes; 4. Reviewing themes; 5. Naming, defining, and theorising themes; 6. Producing a report. This structured approach could easily be applied to the critical reflexive approach.

However, in this study, I identified the discursive patterns of meaning across the interviews by employing an approach to analysis that could be defined as a "sensitivity to language rather than as a 'method'" (Parker, 2004, p. 310). This more fluid analytic process involves identifying common themes and sub-themes while also paying attention to contradictions and outliers, returning to, re-organising, and refining these themes repeatedly to identify "underlying systems of meaning" (Taylor & Ussher, 2001, p. 297). The critical reflexive process involves analysing reflexive journal entries as data alongside interview transcripts and using the two kinds of data together to inform the interpretation.

I chose to organise my data without the use of qualitative analysis software like NVivo, which can be used to assist with the process of organising data into themes. Indeed, the critical reflexive analysis I propose requires commitment to attending closely to the often-implicit ways in which language and power operate in the text as well as a commitment to keeping the narratives whole as much as possible. I, like Braun and Clarke (Braun et al., 2019; Braun and Clarke, 2006) find that this is more easily achieved without the use of software. However, this is a personal preference rather than an imperative of the approach to analysis.

Concluding thoughts: theoretical eclecticism and the process of unknowing

The critical reflexive approach is grounded within a social constructionist epistemological framework. It is an assemblage of predominantly poststructuralist and psychoanalytic theories and practices. Putting these theories and methods carefully in conversation with one another provides the theoretical foundations and the methodological tools to interrogate how broader social structures shaped the individual anxieties and desires of both the researcher and participant, and to capture how these manifest and are reproduced in the interview encounter.

Theoretical eclecticism underpins all aspects of this critical reflexive research approach. Gavey, arguing for the value of theoretical impurity, warns how strict theories and methods tend to discipline our thinking, becoming "boxes that limit and circumscribe research, rather than offering fluid pathways for creating inquiry" (2011, p. 186). Gavey acknowledges the value of transgressing borders of theoretical approaches through careful adaptation and combination:

> I would rarely choose to say "I do discourse analysis" because I prefer to think about research as a process of asking theoretically informed questions – sometimes as much about unknowing as knowing – rather than as the application of a particular method.
>
> *(Gavey, 2011, p. 187)*

This notion of research being a process of *unknowing* is a powerful one. It fits into a feminist poststructuralist agenda of doing the work of unknowing what we take for granted about ourselves and others. We commonly think of research as a process of knowing, it is the process we follow for knowing (more) about the topic we study. The idea of research being a process of unknowing resonates strongly with the critical reflexive approach and with this particular research project. The approach is partly about unknowing what hegemonic research traditions take for granted about the ideals of researcher objectivity and detachedness from the research process. Very often, as I navigated this research process (from conducting interviews, to writing my research journal, to engaging with the data), what I expected to find, how I expected I would relate to participants in interviews, and what I thought I already knew about the topic and about my own positionality and identity, were disrupted or even upended. Engaging in this critical reflexive research process has raised as many new questions as it has answered about the research process, masculinity, sexuality, and sex work. As I hope you will come to find, this project and this book invites a process of unknowing.

Notes

1 See also Helen Kara's excellent video that provides clear definitions of Methodology, Ontology, and Epistemology.
2 Because IM interviews were copied and pasted directly into word processor documents, they have not been edited for spelling and language errors.

References

Ahmed, S. (2006). *Queer phenomenology: Orientations, objects, others.* Duke University Press.

Ahmed, S. (2007). A phenomenology of whiteness. *Feminist Theory, 8*(2), 149–168. https://doi.org/10.1177/1464700107078139

Arendell, T. (1997). Reflections on the researcher-researched relationship: A woman interviewing men. *Qualitative Sociology, 20*(3), 341–368.

Attride-Stirling, J. (2001). Thematic networks: An analytic tool for qualitative research. *Qualitative Research, 1*(3), 385–405. https://doi.org/10.1177/146879410100100307

Boonzaier, F. (2006). A gendered analysis of woman abuse. In T. Shefer, F. Boonzaier, & P. Kiguwa (Eds.), *The gender of psychology* (pp. 133–150). UCT Press.

Boonzaier, F. (2017). The life and death of Anene Booysen: Colonial discourse, gender-based violence and media representations. *South African Journal of Psychology, 47*(4), 470–481. https://doi.org/10.1177/0081246317737916

Boonzaier, F., Huysamen, M., & van Niekerk, T. (2020). Men from the "South": Feminist, decolonial and intersectional perspectives on men, masculinities and intimate partner violence. In L. Gottzén, M. Bjørnholt, & F. Boonzaier (Eds.), *Men, masculinities and intimate partner violence.* Routledge.

Braun, V., & Clarke, V. (2006). Using thematic analysis in psychology. *Qualitative Research in Psychology*, 77–101.

Braun, V., & Clarke, V. (2013). *Successful qualitative research: A practical guide for beginners.* Sage.

Braun, V., Clarke, V., Hayfield, N., & Terry, G. (2019). Thematic analysis. In P. Liamputtong (Ed.), *Handbook of research methods in health social sciences* (pp. 843–860). Springer. https://doi.org/10.1007/978-981-10-5251-4_103

Broom, A., Hand, K., & Tovey, P. (2009). The role of gender, environment and individual biography in shaping qualitative interview data. *International Journal of Social Research Methodology, 12*(1), 51–65.

Butler, J. (1988). Performative acts and gender constitution: An essay in phenomenology and feminist theory. *Theatre Journal, 40*(4), 519–531.

Butler, J. (1999). *Bodies that matter: On the discursive limits of "sex".* Routledge.

Butler, J. (2004). *Undoing gender.* Routledge.

Butler, J. (2008). *Gender trouble: Feminism and the subversion of identity.* Routledge.

Collins, P. H. (1990). *Black feminist thought: Knowledge, and the politics of empowerment.* Hymann.

Crenshaw, K. (1991). Mapping the margins: Intersectionality, identity politics, and violence against women of color. *Stanford Law Review*, 1241–1299.

Crossley, M. L. (2000). *Introducing narrative psychology: Self, trauma and the construction of meaning.* Open University Press.

Edley, N. (2001). Unravelling social constructionism. *Theory & Psychology.* https://doi.org/10.1177/0959354301113008

48 Theories, methods, and practice

Foucault, M. (1981). *The history of sexuality, volume I: An introduction.* Penguin Books (Original work published 1976).

Gadd, D. (2004). Making sense of interviewee – interviewer dynamics in narratives about violence in intimate relationships. *International Journal of Social Research Methodology*, 7(5), 383–401.

Gavey, N. (1989). Feminist poststructuralism and discourse analysis: Contributions to feminist psychology. *Psychology of Women Quarterly*, 13(4), 459–475.

Gavey, N. (2011). Feminist poststructuralism and discourse analysis revisited. *Psychology of Women Quarterly*, 35(1), 183–188.

Gill, R. (2008). Culture and subjectivity in neoliberal and postfeminist times. *Subjectivity*, 25(1), 432–445. https://doi.org/10.1057/sub.2008.28

Gottzén, L. (2013). Encountering violent men: Strange and familiar. In B. Pini & B. Pease (Eds.), *Men, masculinities and methodologies.* (pp. 197–208). Palgrave Macmillan.

Grenz, S. (2005). Intersections of sex and power in research on prostitution: A female researcher interviewing male heterosexual clients. *Signs: Journal of Women in Culture & Society*, 30, 2091–2113.

Hall, S. (2001). Old and new identities, old and new ethnicities. In L. Back & J. Solomos (Eds.), *Theories of race and racism: A reader* (pp. 144–154). Psychology Press.

Henriques, J., Hollway, W., Urwin, C., Venn, C., & Walkerdine, V. (2002). Selections from changing the subject: Psychology, social regulation and subjectivity. *Feminism & Psychology*, 12(4), 427–431.

Hollway, W., & Jefferson, T. (2013). *Doing qualitative research differently: A psychosocial approach* (2nd ed.). Sage.

Hook, D. (2008). Articulating psychoanalysis and psychosocial studies: Limitations and possibilities. *Psychoanalysis, Culture & Society*, 13(4), 397–405. https://doi.org/10.1057/pcs.2008.23

Huysamen, M. (2016). Constructing the "respectable" client and the "good" researcher: The complex dynamics of cross-gender interviews with men who pay for sex. *NORMA: International Journal for Masculinity Studies*, 11(1), 19–33.

Huysamen, M. (2020). Reflecting on the interview as an erotic encounter. *Sexualities*, 23(3), 376–392. https://doi.org/10.1177/1363460718811229

Kara, H. (2020, October 13). *Methodology, ontology and epistemology* [Video]. www.youtube.com/watch?app=desktop&v=vvmcoFKOb9M&t=1s

Kazmer, M. M., & Xie, B. (2008). Qualitative interviewing in Internet studies: Playing with the media, playing with the method. *Information, Community and Society*, 11(2), 257–278.

Landy, F., Maharaj, B., & Mainet-Valleix, H. (2004). Are people of Indian origin (PIO) "Indian"? A case study of South Africa. *Geoforum*, 35(2), 203–215.

Lugones, M. (2007). Heterosexualism and the colonial/modern gender system. *Hypatia*, 22(1), 186–219.

Lugones, M. (2010). Toward a decolonial feminism. *Hypatia*, *25*(4), 742–759.

McCall, L. (2005). The complexity of intersectionality. *Signs*, *30*(3), 1771–1800.

O'Connor, H., & Madge, C. (2016). Online interviewing. In N. G. Fielding, R. M. Lee, & G. Blank (Eds.), *The Sage handbook of online research methods* (pp. 416–434). Sage.

Parker, I. (1992). *Discourse dynamics: Critical analysis for individual and social psychology*. Routledge.

Parker, I. (2004). Discourse analysis. In U. Flick, E. Kardorff, & I. Stein (Eds.), *A companion to qualitative research* (pp. 308–312). Sage.

Pini, B. (2004). On being a nice country girl and an academic feminist: Using reflexivity in rural social research. *Journal of Rural Studies*, *20*(2), 169–179.

Pini, B. (2005). Interviewing men: Gender and the collection and interpretation of qualitative data. *Journal of Sociology*, *41*(2), 201–216.

Plummer, K. (1995). *Telling sexual stories*. Routledge.

Presser, L. (2005). Negotiating power and narrative in research: Implications for feminist methodology. *Signs*, *30*(4), 2067–2090.

Riessman, C. K. (2002). Analysis of personal narratives. In J. F. Gubrium & J. A. Holstein (Eds.), *Handbook of interview research: Context & method* (pp. 695–710). Sage.

Riessman, C. K. (2008). *Narrative methods for the human sciences*. Sage.

Rutherford, A. (2018). Feminism, psychology, and the gendering of neoliberal subjectivity: From critique to disruption. *Theory & Psychology*, *28*(5), 619–644. https://doi.org/10.1177/0959354318797194

Sandberg, L. (2011). *Getting intimate: A feminist analysis of old age, masculinity and sexuality* [Doctoral dissertation, University of Linköping]. http://liu.diva-portal.org/smash/record.jsf?pid=diva2:408208

Spronk, R. (2014). The idea of African men: Dealing with the cultural contradictions of sex in academia and in Kenya. *Culture, Health & Sexuality*, *16*(5), 504–517.

Taylor, G. W., & Ussher, J. M. (2001). Making sense of S&M: A discourse analytic account. *Sexualities*, *4*(3), 293–314. https://doi.org/10.1177/136346001004003002

Thumbran, J. (2019, May 26). Paper by South African academics raises spectre of racism in the academy. *The Conversation*. http://theconversation.com/paper-by-south-african-academics-raises-spectre-of-racism-in-the-academy-116612

van Niekerk, T. J. (2019). Silencing racialised shame and normalising respectability in "coloured" men's discourses of partner violence against women in Cape Town, South Africa. *Feminism & Psychology*, *29*(2), 177–194. https://doi.org/10.1177/0959353519841410

Weedon, C. (1987). *Feminist practice and poststructuralist theory*. Blackwell Publishing.

West, C., & Zimmerman, D. H. (1987). Doing gender. *Gender and Society*, *1*(2), 125–151. https://doi.org/10.2307/189945

Wetherell, M. (1998). Positioning and interpretative repertoires: Conversation analysis and post-structuralism in dialogue. *Discourse & Society, 9*(3), 387–412.

Wetherell, M. (2008). Subjectivity or psycho-discursive practices? Investigating complex intersectional identities. *Subjectivity, 22*(1), 73–81.

Willig, C. (2001). *Introducing qualitative research in psychology.* Open University Press.

Winchester, H. P. M. (1996). Ethical issues in interviewing as a research method in human geography. *Australian Geographer, 27*(1), 117–131.

3

REASONS FOR ARRIVING

Confessions, excitement, and intimacy

Introduction

People do not just appear magically at interviews to tell their sexual stories; they arrive to tell them. A person's choice to participate in our research is neither incidental nor is it irrelevant to the research topic itself. When research is about sexual, taboo, sensitive or criminalised topics, participants' reasons for arrival can be of particular relevance. Men who pay for sex are often referred to as "hard to reach" population to research, as they engage in an activity that is criminalised, stigmatised, and often done in secret. Colleagues and friends were indeed sceptical about how I would manage to recruit enough participants for this study. How would I find participants, and why would they agree to talk to me? However, soon after posting the calls for participants on online classified websites, I was inundated with emails from men who were interested in participating. Given that there were no financial incentives for participating, and that participating could have posed risks for participants, it begs the question, why did these men decide to participate?

Central to the critical reflexive approach is understanding our research participants as "arrivals". This involves acknowledging that people arrive for interviews with particular hopes, expectations, or presumptions about the interview and what they might gain from or contribute to it (Sandberg, 2011). Our participants' motivations for arriving to interviews (a seemingly methodological question) can also provide valuable theoretical insight into how they make meaning of

DOI: 10.4324/9781003093602-3

the topics they arrive to discuss. In this chapter, I will demonstrate how reflecting on men's motivations for participating in this study provided insights into, and often mirrored, their motivations for paying for sex. I will discuss participants' motivations for participating in the research across three themes: the interviews as an opportunity to confess, the interview as an opportunity for *jouissance* or libidinal excitement, and the interview as a space to feel heard and emotionally attended to. In discussing each of these themes, I link men's reasons for participating in the interviews to their motivations for paying for sex, highlighting how methodological questions can be theoretically generative.

The interview as a confessional

A useful first step to understanding participants' motivations for participating in our research is to simply ask them about it. I asked all participants why they had decided to take part in my study. The most common reason participants gave was that the interview was as an opportunity to "tell someone" their secrets about paying for sex. As the following examples demonstrate, for most participants having paid for sex was a closely guarded secret, and many said that I was the first person they had ever told.

> It's not something I can really speak about to people generally, so it's nice to be able to tell someone.
>
> *(Denis, 43, white: IM)*

> You the first person I am sharing this with. I can't even talk to a friend of mine coz I have to protect my girlfriend. But I wanted someone to talk to and you just came.
>
> *(Jabu, 28, black: IM)*

> I tell you what I think, we [Indian men] just don't have someone we can trust to tell our life stories to. A stranger might be our best bet.
>
> *(Kyle, 39, Indian: IM)*

Given that paying for sex is illegal in South Africa and is still largely seen as an immoral and taboo activity, it is unsurprising that so many participants felt that they did not have anyone in their day-to-day life whom they could tell about paying for sex. However, research suggests that the majority of men hide that they pay for sex from their family and friends, regardless of the legal status of the sex industry in their region (Huff, 2011). This is because the stigma associated with sex work should be understood through broader meanings of secrecy and shame that surround all kinds of sex that occur outside of normative heterosexual relationships.

In attending to broader discourses around sex and their implications for the research encounter, I draw on Foucault's (1981) *The History of Sexuality*. Foucault suggests that, historically, sexuality has been understood in terms of the *repressive hypothesis*. This is the assumption that, from the seventeenth century onwards, sex and sexuality have been repressed in Western society; Western societies have treated sex as something private and secret that should be confined to the four walls of the legitimate procreative married couple's home. Sex outside of the heterosexual marriage has been constructed as something particularly unspeakable and shameful, and, as Foucault suggests, has been underpinned by a puritanical "triple edict of taboo, nonexistence, and silence" (1981, p. 5). If we apply this repressive hypothesis to our understanding of sex work today, paying for sex falls squarely into a broader imaginary of an unspeakable kind of sexual practice.

The repressive hypothesis can shed light on why participants may have felt that they had no one that they could talk to about paying for sex – paying for sex is unspeakable for many. However, it does not answer the question of why so many men *wanted* to talk about it, and why they chose to do so in these particular interviews. To answer this question, I draw on Foucault's notion of *the confessional*. Although Foucault asserts that sex and sexuality have been constructed as something shameful and "secretive" (1981), he argues for an understanding of sexuality in society that differs from the repressive hypothesis. He suggests that following the social, economic, and cultural rise of the bourgeoisie during the nineteenth century, sex has in fact been talked about a great deal. However, this talking has taken a very specific and constrained format, *the confessional*.

It was a participant named Steve who first helped me to make the theoretical connection between participants arriving for interviews about paying for sex and Foucault's notion of the confessional:

MONIQUE: Why do you think you decided to [do the interview]?
STEVE: Well, I'm a, I've been wondering about that. After I said yes to you which was kind of spur of the moment. Mmm, I thought there is an element of almost catharsis, confessional. And I think a

lot about that because as I said I am an atheist. I think one of the unfortunate consequences of atheism is that we surrender some really good healthy institutions like the confessional, rituals, you know that we can't replace outside the context of religion . . . Anyway, so when I think of motive that came up. The other is curiosity. Who are you and why are you doing this? And I think just the opportunity to spend a couple of hours doing something out of the ordinary. That's always valuable. That's valuable to me. Adds spice to life. (Steve, 57, white: Face-to-face)

When we think of the confessional, the image of the religious confessional is often invoked, in particular the Catholic Sacrament of Reconciliation (more commonly known as Confession). However, Foucault (1981, p. 59) argues that, "Western man (sic) has become a confessing animal". The confessional is not confined to religious spirituality and has made its way into other aspects of everyday modern life. Today we see examples of confessional practices in the justice system, medicine, education, and family relationships, reality TV, social media, and the research interview. The practices of psychiatry and psychotherapy also mimic the structure of the confession, where the patient freely confesses to the therapist in the hopes of experiencing relief, catharsis, or therapeutic change.

From a Foucauldian point of view, what interests Western society most about sex is not the experience of it, but *"understanding* it – talking about desire, analysing it, dissecting it, exploring it" (Behrent, 2021). The confessional is one of the main mechanisms society relies upon for the production of this knowledge and "facts" about sex and sexuality (1981). Foucault suggests that "for us, it is in the confession that the truth and sex are joined, through the obligatory and exhaustive expression of an individual secret" (Foucault, 1981, p. 61). It then makes a great deal of sense that participants might have desired an avenue through which they can confess their secrets about their paying for sex. Indeed, the interview did become a context for the confessional, a space where men could legitimately engage in a discursive ritual that allowed them to speak about the unspeakable. Steve's construction of the confessional as something beneficial, an opportunity for "catharsis", reinforces Foucault's (1981, 1995) assertion that the obligation to confess is so deeply ingrained in our society that we do not perceive it as a form of top-down power that structures and constrains people's actions but rather as a liberating force. It is exactly through this mechanism that bodies are regulated in contemporary society.

The following excerpt from an interview with Sam provides another example of how the interview became a context for the confessional:

> because you have certain beliefs and doing things doesn't change your beliefs, it just knowing it's [paying for sex] against what you believe in, that is a lot of guilt, it sort of feels hypocritical and most people don't want to be hypocritical . . . that's the main guilt. It's also maybe that keeping quiet about it sort of feels deceitful. It's not nice to be deceitful, it's the same as lying. So that's also maybe one of the reasons why I responded to the ad, because it's a way of telling someone [laughs] you know what I'm saying?
>
> *(Sam, 40, white: Face-to-face)*

Sam's narrative provides detailed insight into how he feels about his client identity as he describes the dissonance between his religious beliefs and paying for sex. It is not only paying for sex that makes Sam feel guilty, but also "keeping quiet about it" that presents the "main guilt". Here we see how paying for sex is necessarily secretive action, but it is simultaneously something that *should* be confessed. The opportunity to confess that the interview offers is important for Sam because, simply as a function of telling someone about paying for sex, he becomes a less deceitful person.

Interpreting the interview as a confessional space is likely to be relevant to much research into sexual practices and desires that fall outside of the strict boundaries of normative sexual practices and compulsory heterosexuality. The confessional may also be relevant to research on other behaviours and desires that are understood as deviant, shameful, or taboo, and those where individuals might feel a simultaneous compulsion towards "keeping quiet about it" and an obligation to confess. Regardless of how we design our research or frame our research interviews, when researching behaviours that are connected to feelings of shame and to taboo, secrecy, and silence, we may very well find that our participants arrive to the interview, at least in part, to use it as an opportunity for confession. But what are the implications of the confessional interview for our research?

We must be cognisant of the confessional dynamics emerging within our research interviews because as interviewers we are directly implicated in them. The confessional only has meaning and purpose in as much as there is someone to bear witness or listen to the confession. Foucault (1981) reflects on the power dynamics of this confessional relationship:

> The confession is . . . a ritual that unfolds within a power relationship, for one does not confess without the presence (or virtual presence) of a partner who is not simply the interlocutor but the authority who requires the confession, prescribes and appreciates it, and intervenes in order to judge, punish, forgive, console and reconcile; a ritual in which the truth is corroborated by the obstacles and resistances it has had to surmount in order to be formulated; and finally, a ritual in which the expression alone, independently of its external consequences, produces intrinsic modifications in the person who articulates it; it exonerates, redeems, and purifies him (sic); it unburdens him of his wrongs, liberates him, and promises him salvation.
>
> *(Foucault, 1981, pp. 161–162)*

Participants' confessions are not only about them doing the telling but also about the interviewer bearing witness to their narratives. In the moment of the interview, I became the witness to men's confessions, confessions that the participants were making in the hope of experiencing some cathartic effect – in Sam's case, in the hope of being unburdened from some of the anxieties that he experienced around being "deceitful". Similarly, when asked why he had responded to my advertisement, Gideon (53, white: IM) said, "I also thought it would help clear the guilt". Christo (41, white: IM) said, "one do not get a lot of chances to talk about a taboo like that, so in a way very nice or even liberating". Unam (32, black: IM) said, "I think I mentioned this is like therapy for me! Lol. Guess I also needed to share my secret with someone". These examples demonstrate how, when our research involves sexual practices and desires that fall outside of that which is deemed socially normative, our participants may arrive to confess their secrets in the hopes of catharsis, liberation or absolution from guilt, or in the hope that some kind of therapeutic change might occur.

If we understand the interview as a form of confessional, then we must also recognise that the interviewer holds a position of power within the interviewer–participant relationship. Regardless of how egalitarian our interviewing style may be, or how much power our participants enter the research process with (as these middle-class, middle-aged, male participants did), we command a level of power over our participants because of the nature of the research relationship. As Schwalbe and Wolkomir suggest, "to agree to sit for an interview, no matter how friendly or conversational, is to give up some control and risk having one's public persona stripped away" (2001, p. 206). There were many instances where these power dynamics were evident. After telling me their intimate secrets, participants voiced anxieties about what I had made of their stories and admissions. Therapeutic and psychiatric discourse trickled into participants' talk as they expressed these anxieties. For instance, Ross (30, white: IM) said, "right now you probably think I'm totally mad". Kyle (39, Indian: IM) asked, "What would you say about my sexuality after what you've heard from me?" Here I, as the interviewer, became the expert figure who would make sense of, judge, validate, diagnose, or interpret their confessions, turning them into knowledge.

Unam's justification for participating in the study ("This is like therapy for me") reflects how therapeutic discourse is entangled within the confessional (Foucault, 1981). The therapeutic discourse present in participants' talk suggests that these men have internalised the pathologising understandings of paying for sex. It also hints at the subtle ways in which the boundaries between therapeutic and research interviews may not be as impenetrable as we may like to believe them to be. As a social work student, I was taught that research interviews are not therapeutic interviews, and that to be good at either we needed to ensure that the boundaries and the distinctions between the two are always firmly in place. However, this does not mean that our research interviews will not be imagined or used as therapeutic spaces by our participants. Nor does it mean that we will not be positioned as therapists by our participants.

Carl Rogers, in his influential paper on the *core conditions*[1] of the therapeutic relationship, acknowledges that other kinds of interpersonal relationships may resemble therapeutic encounters:

> It is not stated that psychotherapy is a special kind of relationship, different in kind from all others which occur in everyday life. It will be evident instead that for brief moments, at least, many good friendships fulfil the six conditions.
>
> *(Rogers, 1957, p. 101)*

Following Rogers' argument, in this book, I stress the importance of not just assuming that research relationship is a "special kind of relationship" that is inherently dissimilar to (and immune to transference from) other everyday relationships. There will be moments where our interview relationships *do* resemble other kinds of relationships or where our participants perceive them as such, often despite our best efforts to keep them separate and distinct. We can either ignore these moments of slippage or we can attend closely to them to explore what they tell us about our methodology and how they can help us answer our research questions.

We can ignore the possibility that our interviews may be imagined as therapeutic encounters and that they may resemble them in some ways (they are both sites for the confessional, after all) (Hollway & Jefferson, 2013). But where we notice parallels, it may be more instructive to look to the rich body of knowledge and critiques around the power imbalances inherent in therapeutic relationships, to sensitise ourselves to how similar dynamics and power imbalances may emerge within our research encounters (Hollway & Jefferson, 2013).

That participants used the interview as an opportunity to confess and as a therapeutic space provided valuable insights into how they made meaning of paying for sex. That the interview became a site for a confession for some participants suggests that that they may have understood their paying for sex as sinful or shameful or that it rubbed against their own moral convictions or social identities. While some men framed their paying for sex in wholly positive terms during the interview, actively resisting the stigmatising discourses about clients, the therapeutic language that crept into their talk suggests a more complex story.

That some participants engaged with the interview as though it were a therapeutic space, projecting onto me the role of the therapist-expert, suggests that (consciously or unconsciously) they perceived being a sex work client as something about them that could be "fixed", or that the desire to pay for sex was something that was in need of therapeutic intervention. This reflects dominant understandings of the client as in need of intervention or reform, evident in the "John school" intervention programmes discussed in Chapter 1. This provided insight into how the stigmatising and pathologising discourses around sex work clients, the sex industry, and "non-normative sexual practices" become internalised. That Unam seeks out "therapy" in relation to his paying for sex, that Ross worries that I must think he is "totally mad", and that Kyle assumes I would have a "diagnosis" of sexuality after sharing his desires with me, reflects not only how the stigma around paying for sex was felt and experienced but also how it was deeply *internalised* by some participants.

Attending closely to how participants related to the interview as a confessional provided me with insight into their subjectivities that I may not otherwise have had access to. I could accept that my interviews were always a completely neutral space that existed for the sole purpose of gathering interview data, or I could acknowledge that participants brought their own hopes and expectations and desires to the research encounter. I could deny the ways in which the interview might have resembled a therapeutic space, or I could question and explore what this tells me about the meanings participants make of paying for sex. To employ a critical reflexive approach is to do the latter.

I would like to return to question of power within the confessional relationship. The preceding discussion of the unequal power relationship imbued in the interview-confessional paints a picture of a unidirectional distribution of power with the researcher in a position of power over the participant who comes to confess. However, this does not account for how gender intersects the dynamics of the interview as a confessional (Huysamen, 2020b). Our positionalities as researchers do not supersede or replace our other identities and positionalities, such as our gender, race, class, disability, and neurodiversity; rather, they intersect with our researcher identity in complex ways. While I attend to the question of race and class in Chapter 5, I want to reflect on gender here. That interviews may become confessionals may set women researchers up as both powerful authority figures *and* passive listeners to men's stories and facilitators of their talk, in line with traditional gender roles. According to traditional patriarchal constructions of femininity, women must act as facilitators of men's narratives, empathetic listeners who seldom challenge or critique men's speech (Grenz, 2005; Pini, 2004; Winchester, 1996). This description of what being a "good" woman looks like in patriarchal society very closely resembles the characteristics of a "good" researcher.

Moreover, the stigmatised nature of our research topics can also complicate and feed into the ways gendered power dynamics play out in the interviews. Because of how stigmatised paying for sex is, I felt that participants had placed a considerable amount of trust in me by arriving to interviews. I felt that I had my participants' deepest secrets in my hands as they confessed, which led me to treat them with additional care. Like a good researcher and a good woman, I always asked questions in non-threatening ways and I avoided responding to participants in ways that might have made them feel challenged, uncomfortable, or judged (see also Huysamen, 2016). Looking back on the transcripts, I realise that I seldom directly challenged moments where participants made statements, comments, or gestures that were sexist and racist. I nodded my head or offered an understanding "mmm" to statements that were in contradiction to my own politics. Upon returning to the interview transcripts, I was horrified to realise how I had colluded with my participants in their racism, homophobia, and sexism, and sometimes facilitated the production of these problematic discourses during interviews. Indeed, numerous researchers (Arendell, 1997; Boonzaier, 2014; Gadd, 2004; Gottzén, 2013; Grenz, 2005; Huysamen, 2016; Pini, 2004, 2005; Presser, 2005, 2005; Winchester, 1996) have reflected upon and critiqued how their patterns of relating to their participants reproduced traditional gender roles and perpetuated dominant discourses of masculinity, femininity, and compulsory heterosexuality. As researchers, and witnesses to participants' confessions, we may find ourselves "doing" the same versions of gender we are interested in critiquing.

On the one hand, interviews with men who pay for sex can become contexts where traditional gender roles are performed and reproduced. On the other hand, the interviewer is also the authority figure who makes sense of, judges, validates, or diagnoses their confessions and narratives, or turns them into academic knowledge. Thus, my reflections on the research interview as a form of confessional is a call to think deeply and critically about the complex ways in which power operates in the interview relationship. Identifying where the interview might resemble the confessional – how the participant might become the confessor and the interviewer might become the expert and witness to these confessions – is a tool that can facilitate our interrogation of the complex, shifting, and multidirectional nature of the power dynamics at play in interviews.

The interview as an opportunity for excitement and risk

Arriving to an interview to talk to a stranger about your involvement in a practice that is illegal is potentially risky business. For some participants, the potential risk involved in the interviews was what motivated them to participate. Most participants said that if anyone were to find out about their paying for sex, their marriages, jobs, and sometimes even their friendships would be threatened. In our initial email correspondence, many participants asked me how they could be sure that I was not working with the police and that they would not arrive only to be arrested. Another concern some participants raised was that I could publicly expose or blackmail them once they had admitted to buying sex. However, all the men who raised these concerns chose to participate in the study. Some participants chose to reveal their real names (I suggested that they did not use their real name in correspondence with me) or gave me information that would allow me to easily identify them. For example, one participant chose to start the interview by telling me his real full name, the name of his business, and making me aware that we had a very close mutual connection who knew his wife well (his wife was unaware that he paid for sex). Participants like these were taking risks by participating in these interviews. But what does this risky behaviour tell me about my research participants?

In an earlier study I conducted with men who pay for sex in South Africa (Huysamen & Boonzaier, 2015), I clearly remember a partici-pant arriving at a café for our interview, standing tall and proud in his full police uniform. The policeman chose to do an in-person inter-view in full uniform about his illegal activity and specifically selected this café that was minutes away from the police station where he worked. That this policeman felt able to do so in a country where sex work is fully criminalised speaks volumes to how laws that criminalise sex work protect some parties, including the police, while harming others (Sanger, 2020; Smith & Mac, 2018; Stardust et al., 2021). But it also demonstrates how this participant went out of his way to turn the interview into a particularly risky encounter for himself.

In the following excerpt, Stewart also talks about paying for sex in terms of the risk involved:

STEWART: One thing that did strike me, which made me think a bit about it, was this question of risk-taking. I mean I regard myself as a very conservative, a low-risk-taker.

MONIQUE: Yes, you mentioned that.

STEWART: But, in fact, on reflection I'm probably not. I mean 'cause this is risky for me. This could destroy my reputation.

MONIQUE: Yes, sure, sure.

STEWART: I ride a Harley-Davidson motorbike. I think, I think I take all the reasonable precautions, but it's a risky thing. I walk up steep hills and climb mountains, which is risky. Um, I invest in businesses with no certainty of an outcome. So perhaps, um, the view of um, engaging with sex workers is just an extension of my risk profile to some extent. (Stewart, 67, white: Face-to-face)

In the first section of this narrative, it is unclear whether Stewart is referring to the interview or paying for sex when he says, "this is very risky for me". Either way, it is the risk of being "found out" or exposed for paying for sex that participants like Stewart find gratifying or get a thrill from. This risk-taking is also tied up with how Stewart constructs his masculinity. He likens this risky behaviour to other stereotypical characteristics of hegemonic masculinity, such as riding a motorbike, taking calculated risks in business, and being physically active and strong. Here, paying for sex adds to Stewart's "risk profile" and his ability to imagine himself according to traditional notions of idealised masculinity (Connell, 2005).

With the sense of risk comes an equally thrilling sense of excitement for some participants. Frank (2003, p. 68), in her ethnographic research in strip clubs, reflects upon how one of her participants said that he enjoyed the thrill of frequenting "dive" strip bars in dangerous parts of town because of the potential risks involved. This participant fantasised about a "worst case scenario" where Frank might not be a researcher and would drug him and rob him. Similarly, Humphreys' (1975, p. 120) controversial study found that middle-class married men derived the same kind of thrill from engaging in oral sex with unknown men in public restrooms, suggesting that "to them, the risks of arrest, exposure, blackmail, or physical assault contribute to the excitement quotient". In my study, participating in the interviews and paying for sex seemed to involve this "excitement quotient" for many participants too.

Many participants articulated their decision to participate in interviews in terms of doing something "out of the ordinary" or "exciting". In the following, Johan talks about the sense of libidinal excitement that he derived from participating in the interview:

It creates some excitement for me as well chatting to you about it, saying this is how my brain works. So, excuse me for that . . . So, ja,[2] it's exciting for me, to answer your question.

(Johan, 48, white: Face-to-face)

The notion of doing something "out of the ordinary" as a reason for participating in interviews is pertinent because this is also why many of these men said they paid for sex. As found in previous studies (Gould & Fick, 2008; Holzman & Pines, 1982; Huysamen & Boonzaier, 2015; Joseph & Black, 2012), many participants in long-term relationships said that paid sex offered them an opportunity to engage in the kinds of sex acts (like anal sex, oral sex, sex with multiple partners, and sex in various sexual positions) that they could not do with their partners. For instance, Bongi (35, black: IM) said he first started paying for sex because of "wanting to get what was forbidden at home, i.e., styles like Blowjobs, Anal and Threesomes". Piet (36, white: IM) said, "with a working girl, you are allowed to experiment with different stuff! Not at home! At home, the same positions/procedures are ALWAYS followed". Paying for sex gave men a thrill because it offered something different and out of the ordinary; it also gave them the opportunity to engage in the kinds of sex acts that they constructed to be "forbidden" or not "allowed" by their wives or partners.

Participants' narratives reflected a broader tendency among men to position women according to the Madonna–Whore dichotomy, where women are constructed either as pure, respectable, nurturing maternal figures (the Madonna) or as sexually promiscuous and deviant whore figures (Bareket et al., 2018; Hollway, 2001; Seal & Ehrhardt, 2003). Imagining their wives as respectable Madonna figures with whom they were only allowed to have mundane "meat and potato sex", as Richard put it, allowed them to imagine the kind of "porn star" sex they had with sex workers as deviant, transgressive, andexciting. When participants told me that they paid for sex because they could not get "porn-star-style" sex from their wives, I tended to follow up with a question about whether they had ever asked their wives to have this kind of sex with them. Although some men said that they had, many said they had never asked and would never ask that of their wives. This strict splitting – imagining their wives as lacking all desire for "porn star sex" – was important in order for their wives to remain, in their minds, pure and respectable women, and for sex with sex working women to remain exciting and deviant. These findings suggest that men pay for sex not only because sex workers are "different" from their wives, but also because paying for sex helps to maintain this difference. These polarised representations of women continue to police women's bodies and limit their sexualities.

They also actively reinforce whorephobia and the stigmatisation of sex workers in society (Bareket et al., 2018; Simpson, 2021).

Be it in arriving for the interview about paying for sex or for a paid sexual encounter, the thrill that men derived from doing something that deviated from their "ordinary" lives, or from what they are "allowed to do", or that posed the risk of discovery was central. This thrill could be understood in terms of the Lacanian concept of *jouissance*. Hook (2017, p. 607) defines *jouissance* as a kind of "negative pleasure", an "intense libidinal arousal", or "getting off" that we derive from doing or thinking things that transgress moral laws or socially prescribed limits. Lacan (2013, p. 177) articulates the transgressive quality of *jouissance*, stating that "without transgression there is no access to jouissance". Hook (2017, p. 607) argues that *jouissance* is tied to pain and horror ("enjoyment intermingled with suffering") because it is often in the moment of being horrified or distressed by our own actions or thoughts that we are also thrilled by them. Whether something is deemed morally, socially, or legally wrong, or contradicts our own personal beliefs, is the very condition that allows us to derive a thrill or enjoyment from it (Hook, 2017; Lacan, 2013).

Part of the allure of paying for sex for some may be related to the *jouissance* or thrill of doing something that transgresses personal, moral, or social boundaries. In an excerpt presented in the previous section, Sam (40, white: Face-to-face) talks about the guilt he experiences in relation to paying for sex, saying, "because you have certain beliefs and doing things doesn't change your beliefs, just knowing it's against what you believe in, that is a lot of guilt". If we apply the Lacanian thesis to this narrative, it is precisely because Sam's religious beliefs condemn paying for sex, and his doing so in spite of these beliefs, which allows for this "kick", "negative pleasure", or *jouissance*.

The pleasure that men derive from paying for sex is, in and of itself, political and discursive. Hook (2017, p. 609) argues that

> the making of laws produces the very conditions of possibility for enjoyment. That is to say, there is a direct relationship between what moral law insists *we not do* and the perverse kick we get out of doing it anyway.

This suggests that it might be precisely the social, moral, legal, and religious discourses that condemn and stigmatise paying for sex that allow it to be thrilling (Holzman & Pines, 1982; Sanders, 2012). This connection is directly relevant to South Africa, where the sex industry continues to be criminalised despite decades of lobbying for legal reform.

Attending closely to the seemingly methodological question, "why did these participants arrive for interviews?" sensitised me to the elements of excitement and risk that men actively sought from the interview process. In the section that follows, I discuss participants' desire for intimacy and connection as the final "reason for arriving" to interviews.

Reasons for arriving: intimacy and connection

There was a resounding sense of loneliness present in many participants' narratives, as men expressed feeling isolated in their marriages or disconnected from their partners. It was this sense of loneliness, I discovered, that also brought some men to the interviews. Some men arrived for interviews with the hope that the interview would meet an emotional need, be it for companionship, conversation, attention, or intimacy.

An interview with a participant called Cyril stands out as a particularly pertinent example of this interviewer–participant dynamic. Cyril was emotionally demanding throughout our interview. He expressed desperation to maintain a connection with me after the interview:

CYRIL: I'm going to be really, really truly honest with you and to the point. I'm actually sorry to hear that you're involved. Okay and there's a reason for me saying this. Okay because I would've so much liked to have had the freedom, okay, to be able to phone you and say: "Monique let's go and have supper or let's go and have lunch and sit and talk to you like I have spoken to you now". Okay. Because, I have never found someone like this. Okay. And I, I don't think that I will find another.

MONIQUE: No, I'm sure that you will. You just need to find them.

CYRIL: It would've been absolutely beautiful, okay, to be to be able to have this freedom. To pick up a phone and say to you: c'mon please, we're such good friends, let's just sit down now. I need to chat about this. Give me your views on it . . . I reiterate and I'm asking you, please don't just cut it. Don't go away from here and just and cut it. I just want you to just drop me a line . . . about any bullshit, irrespective, irrespective of what it is, you know.

Even if it's a bit cold today, what do you think? Because it's food, it's life, it's food. And it it's so, ja it's so, it's so beautiful and, you know I often say to people you know a connection between two people brain-wise, okay is far greater than, connection, anything else. Strangely enough okay . . . I'm not saying that you have got a connection with me. I'm saying that I have got a connection with you. (Cyril, 53, white: Face-to-face)

The way Cyril related to me in the interview tells us something about his desire for intimacy and closeness. Cyril transferred onto me his desire to have someone who would offer him companionship and would be available to attend to his emotional needs when they arose. Cyril also brought to the interview his anxieties about getting older and no longer being desirable to younger women, as he asked me in this same interview whether I would consider getting involved with someone of his age.

Cyril's demands had a significant impact on me during the interview. In my research journal I reflect:

> As the interview with Cyril progressed, I found myself growing more and more mentally fatigued, I was surprised by my strong desire to escape the interview, which seemed to go on forever.

My response to Cyril was quite unusual. I usually felt some affinity towards and connection with most of the participants (another interesting dynamic). Upon a deeper analysis of the interview transcript and of my research journal, I realised that this strong and quite unusual response I felt towards Cyril had something to do with how emotionally demanding Cyril had been throughout the interview. He was one of the participants with whom I had the least rapport, and with whom I spent the most time trying to maintain my boundaries. If I were to draw on psychoanalytic language and concepts here to assist the reflexive process, I would say Cyril transferred onto me his need to be known, accepted, and desired.[3] Due to my own anxieties and defences, I strongly disidentified with and rejected him. Indeed, Cyril seemed to have some awareness of this dynamic between us as he says, "strangely enough . . . I'm not saying that you have got a connection with me. I'm saying that I have got a connection with you". At face value, I found this an odd statement, and after the interview I kept returning to these words. Surely by definition, "connection" implies that two parts are connected to one another. However, this statement went on to be important for my understanding of the nature of men's expectations of intimacy within the paid sexual encounter, upon which I will elaborate later in this chapter.

The following excerpt provides another example of how men's reasons for participating in interviews shed light on the meanings that they make of paid sexual encounters. Johan attributes his participating in the interview *and* his paying for sex to a deep sense of loneliness. He understands his participation in the interview and paying for sex as "going out and finding someone you can talk to":

JOHAN: Ja, and when you getting older, I'm forty-eight next week and you realise but what is money? What is all that materialistic stuff when you don't have love? When you don't have that connection? If you don't feel someone's skin on your skin? That's what love is about and I've missed that boat. That's how I feel. Married for twenty-five years you, you don't feel that emotional connection. There was many days that I wanted to walk out and say I hope that she finds someone that's really, really good for her but you still feel that responsibility. You can't walk out.

MONIQUE: Towards her?

JOHAN: To her, ja, ja. She lost her voice, vocals about five years ago as well. She had laryngitis, so she only has about thirty percent left of the vocals. I'm an outspoken guy, you see me here. . .

MONIQUE: Ja, that's difficult.

JOHAN: So it's a bit of a challenge. And so that's for me, going out and finding someone you can talk to and that's one of the reasons why I'm here as well.

MONIQUE: So do you think that's the reason that you pay for sex, from what you've said you know it's quite a, almost a loneliness on one side within your. . .

JOHAN That's what it is.

MONIQUE: . . . so is it just that responsibility you think that's made you, not ten years ago, decide maybe it would be better to leave?

JOHAN: Maybe responsibility and, and to still have that father-mother house structure. I went to class meetings some years ago and we were the only ones that were still married. So that was a concern . . . That loneliness for me, that intimacy and I said it now you must stop me please.

MONIQUE: No, no, please.

JOHAN: That loneliness where you feel you need that intimacy. Where you need that touch of someone. Someone, you know they don't care, you know that actually it is in your mind, for that hour they care. And you have that skin on skin touch and that girlfriend experience or whatever and you walk away and you, you feel stimulated again. It's how I feel. (Johan, 48, white: Face-to-face)

Johan's narrative suggests that by secretly paying for sex, rather than leaving his wife for another partner, he is able to access the intimacy he desires without having to destabilise the idealised nuclear family unit or threaten the illusion of the monogamous heterosexual marriage (or his identity as a "good" father and husband). Johan's narrative also reflects the resounding sense of loneliness that featured in many men's stories. He speaks regretfully about emotional aspects such as "connection" and "love", as well as the physical aspects of touch and closeness that are amiss in his marriage. Other participants also spoke about using the paid sexual encounter to compensate for their loneliness and to meet these needs for conversation, companionship, intimacy, and physical touch. I have written in more depth elsewhere (Huysamen, 2019a, 2020a) about the kinds of emotional needs and desires men brought to their paid sexual encounters.

While the desire for intimacy and authenticity were central to many men's motivations for paying for sex, most of these men made marked distinctions between the nature of the intimacy in commercial relationships and their "real" non-commercial sexual relationships. For example, in the excerpt earlier, Johan explains that, while the women he pays for sex "do not really care" for him, for the hour that he is with them he is able to imagine that they do. Similarly, Richard said, "I for one like the intensity and the intimacy to go with the physical. I accept and I want it to be manufactured". Richard's assertion that he not only accepts but also wants the intimacy between the sex worker and himself to be manufactured provides important insights into what it is that some men are buying when they pay for sex. That some men are aware of or prefer that women manufacture or perform emotions and expressions of intimacy towards them, suggests that these kinds of time-limited experiences of intimacy and closeness are consciously sought by some men who pay for sex. Previous research on clients has linked Hochschild's (2003, 2012) concept of *emotional labour* to paid sexual encounters (Chen, 2005; Holzman & Pines, 1982; Huysamen, 2019; Sanders, 2008). *Emotional labour* can be defined as the work involved in evoking, shaping, or suppressing emotions, thoughts, behaviours, and expressive gestures in order to meet the requirements of a job (Hochschild, 2003). Part of the emotional labour that sex workers perform involves expressing sexual pleasure as well as genuine interest in, or desire for, their clients (Bernstein, 2007).

Bernstein (2001) uses the term *bounded authenticity* to argue that paying for sex is appealing to some men because it provides the intimacy of a genuine relationship, but within boundaries that insulate them from the obligations commonly associated with heterosexual relationships. In light of these theoretical concepts, Cyril's seemingly counter-intuitive assertion that, "I'm not saying that you have got a connection with me. I'm saying that I have got a connection with you" suddenly makes a great deal more sense. Cyril does not want me to want or demand anything emotionally from him, he only has a desire to make emotional demands upon *me*. Cyril's seemingly contra-dictory statement had puzzled me at first, but upon further reflection it allowed me to better understand, and perhaps even expand upon, the concept of bounded authenticity. This reflects the ways in which the interview relationship dynamics and men's talk about their moti-vations for paying for sex shed light upon one another.

Concluding thoughts

This chapter has coalesced around participants' reasons for arriving to our research. What has motivated our participants to participate in our research, and with what expectations, anxieties, and hopes for the research have they arrived? This chapter demonstrates how the answers to these seemingly methodological questions can provide important theoretical insights.

Attending to participants' motivations for participating in my inter-views not only revealed complex interviewer–participant dynamics operating in the study, but it also provided rich insight into the ways in which men make meaning of their paid sexual encounters. For exam-ple, the finding that men saw the interview as an opportunity to "tell someone" and confess about paying for sex is both methodologically and theoretically important. In the first instance, understanding the interview as a confessional is a call to think deeply and critically about the ways in which power operates in the interview relationship. This is a tool that can facilitate our interrogation of the complex, shifting, and multidirectional nature of the power dynamics at play. At the same time, that participants used interviews as a space to confess about paying for sex also provided deep insight into how men internalised the stigma and pathologising discourses surrounding clients of sex work. Though we often approach our research method and the theory we generate from our data as separate considerations, this chapter highlights the importance of understanding how the methodological and the theoretical are inextricably linked. Interview dynamics (i.e. methodological concerns) will tell us something about our subject matter, and our subject matter will shape the kinds of methodological considerations and challenges we encounter.

Understanding our participants as people who have "arrived" for interviews, rather than as research subjects who have magically and mysteriously appeared before us, means accepting that our participants have considered the destination before setting off. It means acknowledging that they had imagined some purpose or reason for going there (even if that is just a little bit of adventure and excitement), and that they may have expectations and hopes for what might happen when they arrive. It is to acknowledge that they will have some anxieties or reservations too. That our participants have arrived for the interview, why they have arrived, what their hopes and expectations for the interview are, and the relationship dynamics that unfold between participant and researcher is part of the research context. This context is inseparable from the data.

As researchers, we too are arrivals. We have arrived at our research areas and interests, and we continue to arrive to each individual interview, with our own expectations and anxieties. As Ahmed (2006, p. 39) writes, "at least two entities have to arrive to create an encounter". Reflecting only on our participants' motivations, expectations, desires, and anxieties is to tell only half the story. Therefore, in the next chapter, I attend to the conditions under which I arrived at the research.

Notes

1 Rogers's (1957, p. 95) core conditions are: "1. Two persons are in psychological contact. 2. The first, whom we shall term the client, is in a state of incongruence, being vulnerable or anxious. 3. The second person, whom we shall term the therapist, is congruent or integrated in the relationship. 4. The therapist experiences unconditional positive regard for the client. 5. The therapist experiences an empathic understanding of the client's

internal frame of reference and endeavours to communicate this experience to the client. 6. The communication to the client of the therapist's empathic understanding and unconditional positive regard is to a minimal degree achieved".

2   "Ja" is a South African colloquial expression used to affirm or agree, equivalent to "yeah" in English.

3   Cyril transferred his desires to be known, accepted, and desired onto me much in the same way that a client in a therapeutic relationship might do. See Birch and Miller's (2000) article on the parallels between interviews and therapeutic encounters.

References

Ahmed, S. (2006). *Queer phenomenology: Orientations, objects, others.* Duke University Press.

Arendell, T. (1997). Reflections on the researcher-researched relationship: A woman interviewing men. *Qualitative Sociology, 20*(3), 341–368.

Bareket, O., Kahalon, R., Shnabel, N., & Glick, P. (2018). The Madonna-Whore dichotomy: Men who perceive women's nurturance and sexuality as mutually exclusive endorse patriarchy and show lower relationship satisfaction. *Sex Roles, 79*(9), 519–532. https://doi.org/10.1007/s11199-018-0895-7

Behrent, M. (2021, September 30). The true Foucault. *Dissent Magazine.* www.dissentmagazine.org/online_articles/the-true-foucault

Bernstein, E. (2001). The meaning of the purchase desire, demand and the commerce of sex. *Ethnography, 2*(3), 389–420.

Bernstein, E. (2007). Sex work for the middle classes. *Sexualities, 10*(4), 473–488.

Birch, M., & Miller, T. (2000). Inviting intimacy: The interview as therapeutic opportunity. *International Journal of Social Research Methodology, 3*(3), 189–202.

Boonzaier, F. (2014). Methodological disruptions: Interviewing domestically violent men across a "gender divide". *NORMA: International Journal for Masculinity Studies, 9*(4), 232–248.

Chen, M. H. (2005). Contradictory male sexual desires: Masculinity, lifestyles and sexuality among prostitutes' clients in Taiwan. *Travail, Genre et Societes, 10*, 107–128.

Connell, R. W. (2005). *Masculinities* (2nd ed.). Polity Press.

Foucault, M. (1981). *The history of sexuality, volume I: An introduction.* Penguin Books (Original work published 1976).

Foucault, M. (1995). *Discipline and punish: The birth of the prison* (Sheridan, A., Trans.). Vintage (Original work published 1975).

Frank, K. (2003). "Just trying to relax": Masculinity, masculinizing practices, and strip club regulars. *The Journal of Sex Research, 40*(1), 61–75.

Gadd, D. (2004). Making sense of interviewee – interviewer dynamics in narratives about violence in intimate relationships. *International Journal of Social Research Methodology, 7*(5), 383–401.

Gottzén, L. (2013). Encountering violent men: Strange and familiar. In B. Pini & B. Pease (Eds.), *Men, masculinities and methodologies.* (pp. 197–208). Palgrave Macmillan.

Gould, C., & Fick, N. (2008). *Selling sex in Cape Town: Sex work and human trafficking in a South African city.* Institute for Security Studies.

Grenz, S. (2005). Intersections of sex and power in research on prostitution: A female researcher interviewing male heterosexual clients. *Signs: Journal of Women in Culture & Society, 30,* 2091–2113.

Hochschild, A. (2003). *The commercialization of intimate life: Notes from home and work.* University of California Press.

Hochschild, A. (2012). *The outsourced self: Intimate life in market times.* Henry Holt & Company.

Hollway, W. (2001). Gender difference and the production of subjectivity. In M. Wetherell, S. Taylor, & S. J. Yates (Eds.), *Discourse theory and practice: A reader* (pp. 272–284). Sage.

Hollway, W., & Jefferson, T. (2013). *Doing qualitative research differently: A psychosocial approach* (2nd ed.). Sage.

Holzman, H. R., & Pines, S. (1982). Buying sex: The phenomenology of being a john. *Deviant Behavior, 4*(1), 89–116.

Hook, D. (2017). What is "enjoyment as a political factor"? *Political Psychology, 38*(4), 605–620.

Huff, A. (2011). Buying the girlfriend experience: An exploration of the consumption experiences of male customers of escorts. *Research in Consumer Behavior, 13,* 111–126.

Humphreys, L. (1975). *Tearoom trade.* Aldine.

Huysamen, M. (2016). Constructing the "respectable" client and the "good" researcher: The complex dynamics of cross-gender interviews with men who pay for sex. *NORMA: International Journal for Masculinity Studies, 11*(1), 19–33.

Huysamen, M. (2019). Queering the "straight" line: Men's talk on paying for sex. *Journal of Gender Studies, 28*(5), 519–530. https://doi.org/10.1080/0 9589236.2018.1546570

Huysamen, M. (2020a). "There's massive pressure to please her": On the discursive production of men's desire to pay for sex. *The Journal of Sex Research, 57*(5), 639–649. https://doi.org/10.1080/00224499.2019.1645 806

Huysamen, M. (2020b). Reflecting on the interview as an erotic encounter. *Sexualities, 23*(3), 376–392. https://doi.org/10.1177/1363460718811229

Huysamen, M., & Boonzaier, F. (2015). Men's constructions of masculinity and male sexuality through talk of buying sex. *Culture, Health & Sexuality, 17*(5), 541–554.

Joseph, L., & Black, P. (2012). Who's the man? Fragile masculinities, consumer masculinities, and the profiles of sex work clients. *Men and Masculinities, 15,* 486–506.

Lacan, J. (2013). *The ethics of psychoanalysis 1959–1960, book VII: The seminar of Jacques Lacan*. Routledge (originally published in 1986).

Pini, B. (2004). On being a nice country girl and an academic feminist: Using reflexivity in rural social research. *Journal of Rural Studies, 20*(2), 169–179.

Pini, B. (2005). Interviewing men: Gender and the collection and interpretation of qualitative data. *Journal of Sociology, 41*(2), 201–216.

Presser, L. (2005). Negotiating power and narrative in research: Implications for feminist methodology. *Signs, 30*(4), 2067–2090.

Rogers, C. R. (1957). The necessary and sufficient conditions of therapeutic personality change. *Journal of Consulting Psychology, 21*(2), 95–103.

Sandberg, L. (2011). *Getting intimate: A feminist analysis of old age, masculinity and sexuality* [Doctoral dissertation, University of Linköping]. http://liu.diva-portal.org/smash/record.jsf?pid=diva2:408208

Sanders, T. (2008). Male sexual scripts: Intimacy, sexuality and pleasure in the purchase of commercial sex. *Sociology, 42*(3), 400–417.

Sanders, T. (2012). *Paying for pleasure: Men who buy sex*. Routledge.

Sanger, C. (2020). S v Mthethwa: Justice for sex workers in the face of criminalisation? *Agenda, 34*(1), 117–123. https://doi.org/10.1080/10130950.2019.1692514

Schwalbe, M., & Wolkomir, M. (2001). Interviewing men. In J. F. Gubrium & J. A. Holstein (Eds.), *Handbook of interview research: Context and method* (pp. 203–219). Sage.

Seal, D. W., & Ehrhardt, A. A. (2003). Masculinity and urban men: Perceived scripts for courtship, romantic, and sexual interactions with women. *Culture, Health & Sexuality, 5*(4), 295–319.

Simpson, J. (2021). Whorephobia in higher education: A reflexive account of researching cis women's experiences of stripping while at university. *Higher Education*. https://doi.org/10.1007/s10734-021-00751-2

Smith, M., & Mac, J. (2018). *Revolting prostitutes: The fight for sex workers' rights*. Verso Books.

Stardust, Z., Treloar, C., Cama, E., & Kim, J. (2021). "I wouldn't call the cops if I was being bashed to death": Sex work, whore stigma and the criminal legal system. *International Journal for Crime, Justice and Social Democracy, 10*(3), 142–157. https://doi.org/10.5204/ijcjsd.1894

Winchester, H. P. M. (1996). Ethical issues in interviewing as a research method in human geography. *Australian Geographer, 27*(1), 117–131.

4

DEFENCES AND DESIRES IN THE RESEARCH ENCOUNTER

Introduction

Cupples (2002, p. 388) argues that,

> Acknowledging the impact of sex and sexuality on fieldwork is fraught with complexities. However, ignoring our sexuality will not make it go away, but will simply impede our understandings of how it shapes our positionality in a number of contradictory ways.

As researchers, our gendered and sexual identities are always relevant, and in sex research they often become more explicitly central to the research process. This chapter puts forward a central supposition of the critical reflexive approach: that the interviewer and the participant are embodied *sexual subjects* and *defended subjects* who bring both defences and desires to interviews about sex, and that these defences and desires penetrate the interview relationship and shape the data that are produced there. Drawing on examples from interviews with three participants, I demonstrate this approach in action and build a case for the theoretical, ethical, and methodological value of acknowledging that interviews about sex are not neutral and sterile spaces, and that they are not devoid of all sexual feeling, responses, and emotions.

Theorising interviewer and participant as sexual subjects

As sex researchers, we call on people to come and tell us their sexual stories. We ask them to talk to us about sex, to tell us about their

DOI: 10.4324/9781003093602-4

sexual lives, about what shapes their sexual identities, about what kinds of sex they do or do not do, and with whom they do it. On the one hand, sex is a mundane part of human experience in the sense that many people have sex, in one way or another (Jackson et al., 2010). On the other hand, we live in a society characterised by *sex exceptionalism* where sex is treated as something special, delicate, private, and as something that should be viewed differently to other basic human needs (Webber & Brunger, 2018). Thus, when we ask people to tell us about their sexual lives (particularly when stigmatised practices are involved), we may be asking participants to share some of the most sensitive, private, and deeply personal aspects of their lives with us. Sexual stories may be imbued with secrecy and feelings of shame, guilt, and/or with immense pleasure, excitement, and desire. When we ask participants to tell their sexual stories, we may be asking them to talk about an emotive, value-laden, multisensory phenomena which may all at once be a physical act, an identity, a habit, an obligation, a ritual, a form of resistance, or a secret. When we ask participants to talk about their sexual lives, we are asking them to talk about something that could be inextricably tied to their social identity or their sense of self. It could be the source of their marginalisation and othering, the foundation of their community and inclusion, an emotional trigger, a physiological stimulus, and the source of a range of emotions and responses including pleasure, excitement, suspense, fear, shame, pain, guilt, and pride. The point is that sex is a multi-dimensional, multisensory aspect of human experience and there is often *a lot* tied to it.

As social science researchers, our training often sets us up to assume (and indeed strive to ensure) that participants ought to arrive to interviews about sex bringing only facts and stories about their sexual lives and that they will leave all the associated strong emotions, physiological responses, feelings, desires, and anxieties at home, making for neat, tidy, and sanitary interviews. However, the critical reflexive approach argues for the value of acknowledging that participant *and* the researcher are *sexual subjects* who may arrive to interviews about sex with their own experiences, histories, desires, needs, and responses surrounding sex in all its complex multidimensional, multisensory fullness. When we ask our participants, who are sexual subjects, to come and tell us about their sexual lives they may not simply talk about shame, desire, arousal, fear, guilt, but they may (or may not) experience and feel these in the moment of the interview too. It is in this sense that interviews about sex, which are infused with sexual emotions, anxieties, and responses, can be theorised as *sexual encounters*. Theorising the interview in this way is also acknowledging that researchers are sexual subjects too, who may relate to our participants' stories and to the content of the interviews in ways that elicit similar responses in ourselves. I choose this (possibly controversial) language strategically to highlight the importance of acknowledging the sexual emotions and responses in our interviews about sex, and to resist pressures to portray these interviews in ways that (misleadingly) sanitise and neutralise them.

As social researchers, we are trained to ensure that research encounters are as neutral and bounded as possible. But this does not mean that the interview automatically becomes a completely neutral and sterile environment, as though it were a laboratory setting. Certainly, transparency about the research process and setting boundaries are important for any research. This includes setting boundaries and managing expectations with our participants about the nature and the purpose of the interview about sex. For example, given that I recruited participants online via personals or erotic services sections of classifieds websites, I needed to make it explicitly clear that the interview was for academic purposes and that we would not be hooking up. It is our ethical responsibility to ensure that our participants know exactly what the intended purpose and outcomes of the research are, and what the interview process will entail and what it will not entail. However, doing so does not guarantee that our research encounters will be completely devoid of all sexual emotion. To deny that these feelings and responses may arise in research is to render the researcher unprepared to manage them and unable to learn from them.

Theorising the interview as a sexual encounter also means being cognisant of the ways in which the interview process itself may mimic or resemble certain elements of sexual encounters outside of the interview, and to reflect on what the implications of this may be. For example, in his cyber ethnography of online dating apps, Atuk (2020) argues that recruiting participants online for an interview about sex is not entirely dissimilar to hooking up for sex online. I will discuss how in my study my online recruitment process sometimes resembled the process of arranging casual paid sexual encounters.

By defining sex research interviews as sexual encounters, I do not mean that interviews about sex inevitably lead to sex in the field. In fact my reasoning is to the contrary, as it is misperceptions such as this that frame sex research as "dirty work" (Huysamen & Sanders,

2021; Irvine, 2014; Keene, 2021). Stigmatised understandings of sex research and anxieties (commonly held by the broader research community and research ethics committees) that sex researchers cannot maintain boundaries in their work lead sex researchers to remain silent about the sexual elements of their research encounters when they do occur. This silence in turn renders researchers unprepared when they do arise (Hammond & Kingston, 2014). I draw on feminist decolonial scholar Matatu's work on ethics in sexuality research:

> This position should not be taken as advocating for unbridled boundless sexualisation of the research encounter. Rather we should consider it as an attempt to extend the humanizing orientation of sexuality research and extend this perspective to include the researcher. However, my concern is not to indiscriminately centre the sexuality of the researcher, as that would defeat the aims of research. It is the narratives of the participants that we are most interested in. It is my contention that we may elicit these without de-humanizing the researcher.
>
> *(Matutu, 2019, p. 124)*

Matutu (2019) contends that to silence the researcher's sexuality in order to make some claim to neutrality is to dehumanise the researcher and the interview process. Anticipating, acknowledging, and recognising the sexual feelings, emotions, and responses that may arise within research interviews about sex, and supporting other researchers to do the same, is a humanising process and a matter of research ethics and integrity. Perhaps then, more important than the question of what is to be gained from researchers acknowledging interviews as sexual encounters is the question what stands to be lost if we fail to do so?

Theorising interviewer and the participant as defended subjects

I have argued for the value of acknowledging both researcher and participant as embodied sexual subjects. I now draw on Hollway and Jefferson's (2013) concept of the *defended subject* to theorise researchers and participants as *defended subjects* whose anxieties may impact the research process and the data generated as a result. The theory of the defended subject, informed by psychoanalytic theory, is based on the understanding that in any social encounter people experience threats to their identities and these perceived threats elicit anxiety that people will defend against (Hollway & Jefferson, 2013). The theory starts from the assumption that there are always multiple, and often competing, discourses on any given topic and that people draw on particular discourses and discursive positions and not on others as a way of defending against these feelings of anxiety.

Though it is applicable to all research, I have found that the theory of the defended subject is particularly helpful in working reflexively with interviews about stigmatised sexual practices. Because sex work is stigmatised in society, interviews about sex work are likely to be social encounters where both researchers and participants may perceive particularly strong threats to their identities. When participants arrive to our interviews about stigmatised practices like paying for sex, they implicate themselves in these practices which may threaten their most closely guarded identities. In the case of this study, men defended against perceived threats to their identities as fathers, husbands, respectable community members, and "dignified" men. Later in the chapter, I will demonstrate how sex researchers bring our own anxieties to interviews too.

Defences and desires: examples from the field

The critical reflexive approach involves theorising the interview as an encounter where interviewer and the participant are both sexual subjects and defended subjects who bring their own sexual responses and anxieties to the interview. I have selected three interview excerpts to demonstrate how these dynamics directly shaped and limited the data produced in interviews. The first two excerpts are from interviews conducted online with participants called Dan and Jez. The final excerpt presented in this chapter is from a different study I conducted later with autistic men who pay for sex. Carl's interview provides an important example of how and why the researcher may reflect on their own responses in interviews.

The first two excerpts from interviews with Dan and Jez provide examples where participants overtly expressed sexual emotions or sexualised the interview. However, it is important to note that participants like these were in the minority in this study. Most participants (particularly those whom I met with in person) performed a kind of hyperrespectability, and went out of their way to treat me with "respect", watching their language and acting chivalrously in order to defend themselves from the stigmatised hypersexualised "perverted" or "dirty old man" stereotypes commonly associated with men who pay for sex (see Huysamen, 2016). However, I have selected Dan and Jez's interviews because they are helpful in demonstrating and applying the methodological concepts I put forward in this chapter.

Dan: the interview as a sexual encounter

As researchers, our identities can begin to impact upon our research before our participants even arrive to interviews. In fact, our identities can influence whether they arrive at all. In the following excerpt, I ask Dan why he decided to participate in the interview, and his response shows how his perception of my gender informed his decision to take part in the study.

MONIQUE: One last question I wanted to ask, well you kinda did answer it already, kind of. But what was your experience of having to do this over Skype and to talk about paying for sex?

DAN: I was really nervous as the beginning, but I told you as we were chatting on Locanto and then email I kind of got more into it and it started becoming more erotic for me, um to talk about it. Specially, I mean if you were a guy I don't know if I would have actually spoken to you to be quite honest.

MONIQUE: And why is that? Because I mean a lot of people say that so. . .

DAN: I dunno, I think it's just guys feel more comfortable around a woman.

MONIQUE: Is that the only reason why?

DAN: Um in terms of why I would chat to you?

MONIQUE: Yea, if I was a guy, a male researcher?

DAN: Yea, but like I wouldn't let a guy massage me you know.

MONIQUE: Sure. But this is supposed to be different!

DAN: No, it is to a point, but it's kind of the same mind set, that was my point when I said I would never let a guy massage me. I don't feel comfortable opening up my secure side to a male, um. And I think maybe because opening up and talking about it, talking about my experiences is arousing for me, I definitely wouldn't wanna do it with a guy.

MONIQUE: Sure

DAN: So, yea I didn't expect like this, because it's been quite nice chatting to you, it's been yea, opening up, I've never told people things like that. It's been, um, ah, (silence) a turn-on, I'll probably have to go rub-off after this, um, but it's it been very interesting. You're very engaging and you understand your material quite well, um you're a good listener . . . I think for me it was a two-way street, we both got something.

(Dan, 37, Indian: Skype)

Many participants like Dan said that they would not have participated in the study if I had been a man. Regardless of what we as researchers do to try and ensure that our interviews are neutral spaces where our own positionalities do not impact our research, they inevitably do. And it is quite likely that they will begin to shape the interview before it has even commenced.

When I ask Dan why he would not want to be interviewed by a man, Dan explains that the whole interview process – me initially connecting with him online, speaking about the project over email, and discussing his sexual stories over Skype – had been increasingly erotic for him. Dan acknowledges that, rather than just the telling of his sexual stories being erotic, my presence as a woman bearing witness to them was tied to these sexual feelings. He further expands his point by likening the interview to other sexual encounters like him receiving a massage, another sexual experience he would not like to be having with a man. To this I exclaim, in exasperation, "but this is supposed to be different!" However, Dan responds with the very important point that interviews about sex can be "kind of the same mindset". It is important that sex academics reflect upon the ways in which our interviews may in certain ways resemble the casual sexual encounters participants come to be interviewed about. In this example, I, a woman in my mid-twenties and a "total stranger", connect with Dan through an advertisement placed on the same website he usually browses to meet women to pay for sex (and certainly not a website he uses to meet researchers). We exchange details and discuss terms of engagement via email. Finally, we, two strangers, meet to talk about his sexual experiences over Skype, the same online platform he regularly uses for casual sexual encounters. When I designed the recruitment process and the participant information sheets, I had been very concerned about ensuring that there was no ambiguity around the fact that this was a purely academic interview. But what I had perhaps not stopped to reflect upon was that participants might genuinely treat the interview as an academic exercise and contribute to it as such, and still experience it as a potentially arousing or sexual space.

In the excerpt given earlier, when I exclaim to Dan that the interviews were "supposed to be different", I am stating that participants are "supposed" to treat the interviews as completely dissimilar to the sexual encounters they have come to talk about. When I demand that interviews be different, I am also saying that participants are "supposed" to treat me, first and foremost, like a researcher and not like a woman who could be a sex worker, sexual partner, or an object of desire. However, much to my dismay, my professional researcher identity did not just override my positioning as a woman and as a sexual subject (Arendell, 1997). Almost every participant in this study asked me whether I had ever sold sex, whether I would consider selling sex, or suggested that I should sell sex. For example, Benjamin (22, Indian: IM) asked, "have you thought about actually advertising yourself? You can command a high fee". In retrospect, asking about my own involvement in the sex industry seems like a fair question given that participants were asked to share some of their most guarded secrets about paying for sex. However, I experienced participants' positioning me as someone who could be a sex worker as a threat to my professional researcher identity and this rendered me a defended subject.

Dan's admission that he felt aroused because of the interview and his implicating me in this experience left me feeling discredited and ashamed. Perhaps this is a powerful example of how men's sexualisation of women in work settings can leave them feeling disempowered and discredited (Huysamen, 2020a). It made me question whether I was a "proper researcher" and whether my project was "real" research. I reflect on this threat to my researcher identity and the anxiety it elicited in my research journal:

> My interview with Dan has left me feeling resentful and panicky . . . what do I do with these parts of the interviews, like where Dan says he'll probably go and jerk off after the interview? Surely this doesn't count as data? Could I just exclude these sections of talk from my analysis? Do I have to transcribe them? If people were to read these would they take the rest of my research project seriously? Would they think that, rather than real research interviews, these were just something men used to "get off" over. Is this even a real research project? Am I really interviewing these men or am I just playing into their fantasies?

In retrospect, I would answer my last question in this excerpt as "both" – that it is possible to claim to conduct "real" and legitimate research without having to deny that some participants may experience sexual feelings as a result of participating in that research.

As researchers, we too arrive to interviews with our own expectations, hopes, and anxieties for the interview, and inevitably with our own baggage. I entered the interview as a *defended subject* who felt and guarded against threats to my own identity (Hollway & Jefferson, 2013). I approached the interviews with the expectation that men might sexualise me. I brought with me a personal discomfort and an anxiety that if they did so that it might negate the integrity of my research. As my journal entry reflects, in writing up my findings, I was reluctant to acknowledge men's admission that they had experienced sexual feelings because of participating in my interview. I understand the root of these anxieties as manifold and intersecting. Firstly, my anticipation of men's sexualisation of me was linked to my positionality as a woman. As woman researchers, we bring with us a history of being (both overtly and covertly) sexualised in various spheres of our lives. We learn to anticipate it. We are taught that we can and indeed that we should moderate our behaviours to avoid or control men's sexualisation of us.

Secondly, my response to men expressing sexual feelings, and my anxiety that this would negate my position as a researcher and the credibility of my work, can be attributed to traditional positivist research discourses to which psychology as a discipline largely ascribes, reproduces, and reinforces. Dominant positivist research traditions privilege and uphold the illusion of the researcher as neutral, objective, and detached (Thomas & Williams, 2016). From these positivist epistemological assumptions, failure to "control" for the ways in which extraneous variables may influence our findings, and failure to create a blank laboratory-like context for data collection is to compromise our research. That my participants related to me as a sexual subject rather than as a faceless walking lab coat was to have failed as a (social) scientist. That one's own identity has slipped into the data is to have slipped up.

Thirdly, my position of the defended subject can be understood in relation to the challenges of conducting sex research in the academy, which remains a largely risk-aversive and conservative context (Huysamen & Sanders, 2021). Geographies of sexualities scholars have long critiqued the "squeamishness" of academia, which is inherently erotophobic (Binnie, 2007; De Craene, 2017). Within academia, sexuality research is routinely treated with less respect, viewed with suspicion and scepticism, and understood in terms of risk and vulnerability (Irvine, 2012, 2014; Thomas & Williams, 2016; Webber & Brunger, 2018). Irvine (2014, p. 638) contends that, "Sexuality research is produced as dirty work by the broad university system, and the practices by which this occurs represent institutionalized bias". Sex researchers may enter the research process already having had experiences of having their work undermined and even hindered by their institutions and their colleagues (Attwood, 2010; Fahs et al., 2017; Hammond & Kingston, 2014; Keene, 2021; Simpson, 2021). Myself and others have written about the challenges of seeking ethical approval from institutional research ethics committees for sex research (see Huysamen & Sanders, 2021; Keene, 2021; Simpson, 2021). Thomas and Williams (2016, p. 84) talking about the way in which sex research is approached with prejudice and suspicion within and by the academy suggest that:

> What often happens in response to this suspicion is that many sex researchers tend to fall back on a position of quasi-neutrality where they claim that their scientific objectivity and their positivist methodologies supersede and make irrelevant or at least incidental their own sexual desires.

I read Thomas and Williams as reflecting on how sex researchers are defended subjects who fall back on the position of "quasi-neutrality" to defend the legitimacy of their position as researchers and their work. Cupples (2002) discusses how researchers might avoid acknowledging the sexual elements present in their sex research for fear that these might call into question the credibility of their work. Similarly, Taylor and O'Connell Davidson, reflecting on their experiences of researching sex work, suggest that:

> Prostitution occupies a troubled and troubling space between two very different symbolic domains – the public world of market relations, and the private domain of sexual and domestic life . . . Researchers who enter this space are often conscious that they too may be perceived negatively, that their academic peers may suspect them of having failed to maintain clear boundaries between their "public" professional selves and their "private" sexual selves.
>
> *(2010, p. 50)*

Indeed, my anxieties around the sexual elements of the interview had everything to do with my own need to perform being a professional researcher doing legitimate research in the face of doing the kind of research which is already delegitimised. My discomfort with the possibility of being sexualised, or even simply being acknowledged as a sexual subject, in this way by these particular men who pay for sex, was tied into the fact that in order to protect my identity as legitimate researcher I needed to do "right" kind of femininity to be the "respectable" researcher in the interview.

Crucially, my anxieties and responses to the interview reflect the extent to which sex work is stigmatised, and how this continues to be reflected and reproduced both inside and outside of the academy. Particularly, it reflects the *whorephobia* that operates within our society (Richter et al., 2020). Simpson (2021) defines the term as follows:

> Whorephobia is a term used to describe the hatred, disgust, and fear of sex workers – that intersects with racism, xenophobia, classism and transphobia – leading to structural and interpersonal discrimination, violence, abuse and murder. Whorephobia is deeply embedded within societies and is internalised by people of all genders which functions to regulate (namely women's) sexuality and reinforce traditional bourgeois gendered norms.

As a woman researcher, I embarked on research about sex work against the backdrop of centuries of whorephobia within a patriarchal society that delimits what a respectable woman (not to mention a respectable researcher) can and must do. I chose to research sex work, work that remains taboo and a term that continues to be used as a slur against women today. While Simpson (2021) points out that the stigma sex work researchers face through association is not comparable to the level of stigma experienced by sex workers, conducting sex work research can elicit whorephobic responses that researchers will have to navigate and cope with.

Not only do we need to manage others' prejudiced responses to our research but also our own. Men consistently asking me whether I had or would sell sex was so anxiety provoking for me because, at an unconscious level, I needed to distance myself from the "whore" identity. I needed to prove that I was not doing this research because I sold sex myself or because I was aroused by the thought of doing so.

In this moment, I reproduced the flawed idea of the impossibility of being both a sex worker and a legitimate researcher, painfully reflecting my own internalised whorephobia. Indeed, being reflexive of our research practices can be painful.[1]

My insistence on being positioned as the "respectable researcher" rather than a "whore" reflects and reproduced this whorephobia and the damaging binary discourses or good and bad women that continue to limit, police, and stigmatise women. As Waling articulates, "I am not 'separate' from my research participants. I am part of a broader political fabric constrained by heteronormativity and patriarchy" (2018, p. 725). Thus, when our research elicits defences and our own prejudices surface, we can understand these as, in part, reflections of broader society. We can use them as an opportunity to deepen our understanding of the topics we study, to deepen our understanding of how this stigma and patriarchal systems of oppression operate in the interview encounter, in our own lives, and in broader society.

But what do my defences "do" in the interview and what are the implications for the data produced there? Noteworthy is how I respond to Dan's admission that he had found the interview arousing. Firstly, I make it clear that I do not share these feelings and I reframe the interview by stating that, for me, it is about research. My tone is defensive enough for Dan to feel that he needs to explain that he was not hitting on me but merely sharing the sexual feelings that the research encounter had elicited. When Dan likens being interviewed to another kind of sexual encounter like having a massage, the effects of my defensiveness are evident. Instead of letting Dan reflect upon his motivations and experiences of the interview (which Dan rightly points out is what I had asked him to do), I reject his experiences. I tell him how he is "supposed to" relate to me, refusing to be an object of his desire. However, as researchers we "base our claims to knowledge on the assumption that participants would reveal something of what they are 'really' like to us" (Huysamen, 2020a, p. 385). But when Dan shares something about his sexual subjectivity by admitting that he feels aroused by the interview encounter, it is too much for me to bear. Because of my need to control and contain the interview, Dan expressing his sexual responses when I was implicated in them is unbearable for me.

Jez: consent and coercion in the interview

The next excerpt from an interview with Jez provides insight into the shifting interviewer–participant power dynamics that were at play. Here Jez positions me as a sexual subject and turns the interview into a transactional encounter.

JEZ: We, going into some serious depth now. It's a two-way street. First, I want to know what you enjoy sexually. Not details just basics. Then I will tell you what sparked me to see selective working girls.

MONIQUE: I'm sorry but I don't want to make this conversation about me and my sexuality. I understand that in a way that's a bit unfair, but I have to set some guidelines for my research. . .

JEZ: Ok let me ask basic questions that are common. You can answer yes or no. What I have learnt in my MBA [Master of Business Administration] is that practical experience is what contributes significantly to one's understanding of the theory. Ok here goes. Do you enjoy foreplay as a build up? Oral sex giving and receiving?

MONIQUE: I'm really sorry but with all due respect, I am going to have to end this interview now. . .

JEZ: If you are not open-minded enough to be able to reciprocate with mutual opinion you are wasting your time with this project and it will, believe me, be the difference between a C grade and A grade with distinction. You will never understand a one-sided opinion until you get questioned. (Jez, 45, white: IM)

Grenz (2005, p. 2097) suggests that in our patriarchal heteronormative society, when a woman researcher interviews men about their sexuality, the heteronormative position of the male "looker" and the "looked-at" woman is subverted, positioning women in a way that threatens traditional gendered power relations. It could be suggested that, by focusing the questions back on my sexuality, Jez attempts to return me to my rightful place as the "looked at" rather than the "looker", reasserting his position of power. There were other ways in which men attempted to challenge my position of power within these interviews. For example, men tried to challenge the power that my education afforded me by asserting themselves as equally or more educated or knowledgeable than me. Note how Jez emphasises his own MBA, as well as his patronising tone when he explains how I can get good grades as though this was a school assignment. However, this interview with Jez illustrates how, even though some participants asserted their power in the interviews, I, as the interviewer, had the "final say". In this example, it is I who ends the interview. It is I who continues to have the authority over this exchange right here in this chapter long after his voice has been silenced. This exchange thus illustrates the complex and shifting nature of the power relations within the interview.

In this interview with Jez, I seem to have been, as Gadd (2004, p. 397) reflects in his paper exploring the dynamics between him and a male interviewee, "far more geared towards establishing my intellectual authority, rather than the particular methodological imperatives I adopted". Feminist researchers such as Oakley (1981) have long called for egalitarian interviewing methods that include mutual disclosure. Is it this mutual disclosure that Jez is demanding from me? I, the defended subject, refuse to disclose anything about my own sexuality, despite expecting my participants to do so themselves. I end the interview early, abandoning (some) of my research principles and losing the opportunity to hear Jez's whole story.

This reflection of power within the research encounter brings to the fore some difficult questions about "researching up" (Neal & McLaughlin, 2009) using feminist methods and principles. What are the possibilities and pitfalls for using feminist methods and values, centred on facilitating egalitarian research relationships and empowering participants? In particular, what are these possibilities and pitfalls when participants are like those in this study: white, middle-class, middle-aged men who are not disempowered and disenfranchised in the same ways as the participants for which feminist methodologies were intended? Though we may not have finite answers to these "wicked" methodological problems, applying a critical reflexive approach allows the researcher to grapple with them. This makes for a more self-aware and critical researcher who is in tune with the values and ontological and epistemological assumptions that underpin their research.

Jez's interview also provides some deeper understanding of the dynamics of coercion and consent and the transactional nature of some sex work relationships. In the excerpt presented earlier, Dan hints at the transactional nature of the interview, saying, "I think for me it was a two-way street, we both got something". He is suggesting that I gained my research data (the currency of my work) while he got the opportunity to feel listened to, excited, and aroused. The same reason many men give for paying for sex (Huschke & Schubotz, 2016; Huysamen, 2020b; Sanders, 2012). In the excerpt given earlier, Jez transforms the interview into a transactional encounter but takes a much more coercive and entitled tone. He attempts to use the resources that I need (his narratives) to coerce me into complying with his demands, becoming threatening when I do not "reciprocate". Here, Jez tries to turn my "no" into a "yes" by insisting that my choosing to research men's experiences of paying for sex, I must also be consenting to talking about my own sexuality.

In the months that followed this interview, I repeatedly returned to this encounter and to the question of whether I had "asked for it". Had I asked to be treated in this way and to have these demands made upon me by being a woman choosing to interview men about sex? The lines between consent and coercion become blurred in this research relationship for both Jez and I. The demands Jez makes on the interview relationship reflect the widely held assumptions about transactional relationships: that when sex is paid for, consent is automatically implied and therefore consent neither needs to be explicitly sought and confirmed nor can it be withheld (Huschke & Coetzee, 2019). Reflecting on how these transactional dynamics played out within the interview encounter offered me a deeper understanding of how questions of consent and coercion might be complicated and blurred in transactional relationships outside of the encounter.

Carl: the researcher as the desiring subject

Thus far I have discussed participants' sexual feelings and responses in relation to my positionality as the researcher, and I have reflected on my own defended responses to them. But I have not attended to my own sexual feelings or responses. De Craene (2017, p. 454) notes that even in reflexive accounts of sex research, an analysis of the researcher as the *desiring* subject is often omitted. De Craene argues that including these accounts is of methodological, epistemological, *and* political importance.

The practice of focusing on the erotic subjectivity of the researcher in the field is given voice in Kulick and Willson's (1995) important edited collection on the taboo around researchers talking about personal desire. Some researchers have begun to address the importance, possibilities, radical potential, and challenges of researchers reflecting on their own sexual subjectivities in the field (Allen, 2012; De Craene, 2017; Feliciantonio & Gadelha, 2017; Thomas & Williams, 2016; Waling, 2018). García-Iglesias (2020) reflects upon moments where his interviews with bugchasers (gay men who eroticise HIV) became "charged" with sexual emotion (2020, p. 2). He demonstrates how his own sexual responses within the interview, and how interviewer–participant interactions flipped between fantasy and objective reality, provided insights into the ways in which his participants made meaning of the practice that he would otherwise not have been privy to. Similarly, Waling (2018) provides a detailed account of her ethnographic research of a male strip-tease show for women. She reflects on how her feelings and responses in the field (feelings of guilt, desire, jealousy, and embarrassment) in relation to the male dancers and other women attendees provided insight into how patriarchal and antifeminist ideals continue to operate and be reinforced in this space. These findings go against assumptions of the subversive, antipatriarchal, nature of male strip-tease shows for women. In both examples, researchers' reflexive practices provide them with important new theoretical insight into their subject matter which they do not believe they would otherwise have had access to. This shows how reflexive approaches, which rely in part on the embodied responses, can help generate deeper and more nuanced understandings that dig beneath the surface of what is more obviously said or observed in the field.

Inspired by these texts and debates, I returned to my research journal in search of moments where I reflected upon my own sexual feelings, emotions, or responses during the research process. There were none. What are the reasons for my silence about my own sexual feelings and responses despite the critical reflexive approach I so carefully and intentionally employed? Perhaps there were no such moments in these interviews with these particular men. However, drawing on the understanding of the researcher as the defended subject, to admit a single instance of desire or arousal, albeit in the secrecy of my own research journal, would have been to severely threaten my own identity as a professional researcher. The silences in my research journal suggest that even our own research journals (which are our reflexive methodological tools) are not immune to our defences.

In a more recent study, however, I had been more careful to attend to my positionality as an embodied and sexual subject. In this study, I interviewed 20 autistic men without learning disabilities who had paid for sex about their experiences of intimacy, relationships, and sex to explore how these tied into their motivations for paying for sex. I interviewed Carl, a 24-year-old Dutch heterosexual university student. We had arranged the interview over email and conducted the interview over online video call. In my research journal, I reflect on the encounter:

> The moment the video call connected I was struck by what an attractive, in fact beautiful, man he was. I felt suddenly dreadfully conscious of my own image staring back at me from the corner of the screen. Next to this fresh-faced man (seven years younger than me) with his soft, sad eyes and his freshly ironed and well-fitting grey t-shirt, I instantly felt self-conscious, unattractive, and a little dishevelled. I wished I'd put a little more effort into my appearance before the interview which happened at the end of a long day.

My visceral reaction occurred within the first few seconds of the interview and took me by surprise. I soon gathered myself, regained my confidence, and the interview continued as I may have expected it to. This fleeting moment would have been forgotten had I not taken time to write it down in my research journal. It is important to ask, how is this encounter and this particular emotional reaction to a participant I found desirable significant to the data and the question of autism and intimacy and the challenges participants arrived to discuss? In this interview, Carl spoke articulately and engagingly about his long struggle with depression (which included periods of institutional care), his lack of self-worth, and his debilitating social anxieties. These had had devastating impacts on his ability to initiate and form intimate relationships, which in turn affected his sense of worth. He spoke about how it was painful for him to watch couples of his age walking hand in hand in the summer in Amsterdam, as he knew he would never get to enjoy the same. So low was his self-esteem and strong were his fears of rejection that he could not bring himself to try dating apps, despite wanting to. He was convinced that no woman his age would see his profile and find him attractive enough to "swipe right" and choose to connect with him. If I had merely been reading a transcript of the interview, perhaps I would have taken him at his word and assumed that he presented conventionally unattractive and socially awkward, and that this was partly implicated in his difficulties with intimacy. However, it was my own affective and embodied response – a fleeting moment of being disarmed by his attractiveness that offered me deeper insight into Carl's social and emotional world, his cognitive distortions, and his distorted sense of self. The utter dissonance between how I had seen him and how he believed women saw him provided me with insight into his psychosocial life and his struggles with intimacy, insight that a "neutral" and decontextualised account could not have provided.

Concluding thoughts: reflecting on silences in the interview process

This chapter makes a methodological contribution to the field of sex research by offering an approach to reflexivity that theorises the interviewer and participant as both defended and sexual subjects who bring to interviews their own sexual histories, anxieties, emotions, and desires. It reflects on the complex, multidirectional, and ever-shifting gendered power dynamics that might operate in interviews about sex. It brings to the fore some of the possible dilemmas and contradictions that feminist researchers doing sex research might be confronted with, as we experience tensions between our various positionalities as researchers, as women, and as feminists, and as we come to terms with our own prejudices, defences, and desires. As critical feminist decolonial researchers, we are likely to find ourselves contradicting or working in opposition to our methodological or ideological principles at some point in the research process. Waling (2018, p. 724) reflects on how our various and intersecting identities and positionalities may be "hostile" to one another:

> I realized that to effectively "do" good research, I had to effectively decide what was most important. To be objective and professional, to be the feminist activist, or to be the desiring woman. I realized I could not authentically claim any particular one identity to achieve the said aim. Each facet of my identity was hostile to the others as I attempted to navigate the highly sexualized and gendered space before me. Instead, I had to embrace all three facets of my identity and their contradictions to comprehend the scene before me. I had in a way, failed at performing what I felt was expected to be a good researcher, but I gained in understanding of how highly volatile research can be in a space riddled with complex sexed and gendered power dynamics.

These difficulties, contradictions, and conflicts are never completely avoidable in any research and they might be felt particularly strongly in the sex research. However, we can begin to address these issues by building an analysis of them into our research design. We can choose to silence the sexual feelings, responses, and anxieties operating in our interviews to build a façade of neutrality around our work. But if we do not write and talk about defences and desires in the research process, and we do not consider and offer approaches to work with them, we render researchers who come after us wholly unprepared to manage these dynamics when they do arise. When established sex researchers are silent about these dynamics, new sex researchers run the risk of experiencing feelings of shame, inadequacy, and isolation. Acknowledging that interviews about sex may elicit sexual anxieties, desires, and responses – and training and supporting other researchers to do the same – is professional, ethical, and methodological practice.

However, a commitment to acknowledging rather than silencing the ways in which defences and desires operate in the research encounter does not equate to an obligation for the researcher to make public every moment of every interview. Not all researchers are equally positioned to do so. Not everything that happens in our research encounters – neither participants' stories nor researcher's reactions and responses – automatically belong to the academy (Tuck & Yang, 2013). Giving voice to every interaction and moment in our research encounters is neither automatically best practice nor necessarily the most ethical approach. Practicing critical reflexivity may sometimes mean knowing when to choose to be silent. As Tuck and Yang (2013, p. 224), in their powerful chapter on refusal in research argue, "refusal understands the wisdom in a story, as well as the wisdom in not passing that story on". Similarly, Ahmed, in the foreword for *Secrecy and Silence in the Research Process* (2013), contends that,

> Sometimes silence is a strategic response to oppression . . . one that acknowledges that speech might not be empowering, let alone sensible . . . Sometimes we might stay silent about some of the findings of our research because we do not trust how those findings might be used by other actors.
>
> *(Ahmed, 2013, p. xvi)*

My critical reflexive approach calls for researchers to practice critical awareness and build these interrogations carefully into their methodology. Whether we do so publicly or as a private part of our research process, this means making a space within the research process to identify and understand psychoanalytic dynamics such as the unconscious, defences, and anxieties. It is to explore how they operate in our research to shape, limit, and drive the content of our interviews. It means that, as researchers, we aim to approach our own embodied experiences and those fleeting moments of shame, anxiety, anger, surprise, or desire we may feel in our research encounters as relevant responses that tell us something more about the complex topics we study. Whether we choose to publicly write about these dynamics, engage in critical discussions with our colleagues and students, or reflect on them only in private, we can build a careful and critical reflexivity into the research process, from the development of our research questions through to writing up and dissemination and beyond.

Note

1   See, for example, Ellis's (1995) honest reflection the emotional and ethical quandaries involved in returning to the field to face our participants after publishing research about their intimate lives. Ellis provides a reflexive account interrogating her personal motivations for conducting the research and how her personal anxieties about her own working-class background were tied into her need to construct her participants as Other.

References

Ahmed, S. (2013). Foreword. In R. Ryan-Flood & R. Gill (Eds.), *Secrecy and silence in the research process: Feminist reflections* (pp. xvi–xx). Routledge.

Allen, J. (2012). One way or another: Erotic subjectivity in Cuba. *American Ethnologist*, *39*(2), 325–338. https://doi.org/10.1111/j.1548-1425.2012.01367.x

Arendell, T. (1997). Reflections on the researcher-researched relationship: A woman interviewing men. *Qualitative Sociology*, *20*(3), 341–368.

Attwood, F. (2010). Dirty work: Researching women and sexual representation. In *Secrecy and silence in the research process: Feminist reflections* (pp. 177–187). Routledge.

Atuk, T. (2020). Cruising in the research field: Queer, feminist, and cyber autoethnography. *International Review of Qualitative Research*, *13*(3), 351–364. https://doi.org/10.1177/1940844720939851

Binnie, J. (2007). Sexuality, the erotic and geography: Epistemology, methodology and pedagogy. In *Geographies of sexualities*. Routledge.

Cupples, J. (2002). The field as a landscape of desire: Sex and sexuality in geographical fieldwork. *Area*, *34*(4), 382–390.

De Craene, V. (2017). Fucking geographers! Or the epistemological consequences of neglecting the lusty researcher's body. *Gender, Place & Culture*, *24*(3), 449–464. https://doi.org/10.1080/0966369X.2017.1314944

Ellis, C. (1995). Emotional and ethical quagmires in returning to the field. *Journal of Contemporary Ethnography*, *24*(1), 68–98. https://doi.org/10.1177/089124195024001003

Fahs, B., Plante, R. F., & McClelland, S. I. (2017). Working at the crossroads of pleasure and danger: Feminist perspectives on doing critical sexuality studies. *Sexualities*, 1–17.

Feliciantonio, C. D., & Gadelha, K. B. (2017). Affects, bodies and desire: "Queering" methods and methodologies to research queer migration. *Tijdschrift Voor Economische En Sociale Geografie*, *108*(3), 275–288. https://doi.org/10.1111/tesg.12235

Gadd, D. (2004). Making sense of interviewee – interviewer dynamics in narratives about violence in intimate relationships. *International Journal of Social Research Methodology*, *7*(5), 383–401.

García-Iglesias, J. (2020). The maroon boxer briefs: Exploring erotic reflexivity in interview research. *Qualitative Research*. https://doi.org/10.1177/1468794120927676

Grenz, S. (2005). Intersections of sex and power in research on prostitution: A female researcher interviewing male heterosexual clients. *Signs: Journal of Women in Culture & Society*, *30*, 2091–2113.

Hammond, N., & Kingston, S. (2014). Experiencing stigma as sex work researchers in professional and personal lives. *Sexualities*, *17*(3), 329–347.

Hollway, W., & Jefferson, T. (2013). *Doing qualitative research differently: A psychosocial approach* (2nd ed.). Sage.

Huschke, S., & Coetzee, J. (2019). Sex work and condom use in Soweto, South Africa: A call for community-based interventions with clients. *Culture, Health & Sexuality*, 1–15. https://doi.org/10.1080/13691058.2019.1568575

Huschke, S., & Schubotz, D. (2016). Commercial sex, clients, and Christian morals: Paying for sex in Ireland. *Sexualities*, *19*(7), 869–887.

Huysamen, M. (2016). Constructing the "respectable" client and the "good" researcher: The complex dynamics of cross-gender interviews with men who pay for sex. *NORMA: International Journal for Masculinity Studies*, *11*(1), 19–33.

Huysamen, M. (2020a). Reflecting on the interview as an erotic encounter. *Sexualities*, *23*(3), 376–392. https://doi.org/10.1177/1363460718811229

Huysamen, M. (2020b). "There's massive pressure to please her": On the discursive production of men's desire to pay for sex. *The Journal of Sex Research*, *57*(5), 639–649. https://doi.org/10.1080/00224499.2019.1645806

Huysamen, M., & Sanders, T. (2021). Institutional ethics challenges to sex work researchers: Committees, communities, and collaboration. *Sociological Research Online*, *26*(4), 942–958. https://doi.org/10.1177/13607804211002847

Irvine, J. M. (2012). Can't ask, can't tell: How institutional review boards keep sex in the closet. *Contexts*, *11*(2), 28–33. https://doi.org/10.1177/1536504212446457

Irvine, J. M. (2014). Is sexuality research "dirty work"? Institutionalized stigma in the production of sexual knowledge. *Sexualities*, *17*(5–6), 632–656. https://doi.org/10.1177/1363460713516338

Jackson, S., Scott, S., & Books, D. (2010). *Theorizing sexuality.* McGraw-Hill Education.

Keene, S. (2021). Becoming a sexademic: Reflections on a "dirty" research project. *Sexualities.* https://doi.org/10.1177/1363460720986915

Kulick, D., & Willson, M. (Eds.). (1995). *Taboo: Sex, identity and erotic subjectivity in anthropological fieldwork.* Routledge. https://books.google.co.uk/books?hl=en&lr=&id=-imIAgAAQBAJ&oi=fnd&pg=PR7&dq=taboo,+sex+idenityt+&ots=rmF86-9a1p&sig=UKb6eBGk95nFYpErNruJwT6eokg

Matutu, H. (2019). "On the way to calvary, I lost my way": Navigating ethical quagmires in community psychology at the margins. In *Decolonial feminist community psychology* (pp. 111–128). Springer.

Neal, S., & McLaughlin, E. (2009). Researching up: Interviews, emotionality and policy making elites. *Journal of Social Policy*, *38*(4), 689–707. https://doi.org/10.1017/S0047279409990018

Oakley, A. (1981). Interviewing women: A contradiction in terms. In H. Roberts (Ed.), *Doing feminist research* (pp. 50–61). Routledge.

Richter, M., Wasserman, Z., & Lakhani, I. (2020). Targets of hate, shame or exploitation?: The (violent) conundrum of sex work in democratic South Africa. *International Journal of Critical Diversity Studies*, *3*(1), 9–24. https://doi.org/10.13169/intecritdivestud.3.1.0009

Sanders, T. (2012). *Paying for pleasure: Men who buy sex.* Routledge.

Simpson, J. (2021). Whorephobia in higher education: A reflexive account of researching cis women's experiences of stripping while at university. *Higher Education.* https://doi.org/10.1007/s10734-021-00751-2

Taylor, J. S., & O' Connell Davidson, J. (2010). Unknowable secrets and golden silence: Reflexivity and research on sex tourism. In R. Ryan-Flood & R. C. Gill (Eds.), *Secrecy and silence in the research process: Feminist reflections* (pp. 42–53). Routledge.

Thomas, J. N., & Williams, D. J. (2016). Getting off on sex research: A methodological commentary on the sexual desires of sex researchers. *Sexualities*, *19*(1–2), 83–97. https://doi.org/10.1177/1363460715583610

Tuck, E., & Yang, K. W. (2013). R-words: Refusing research. In D. Paris & M. T. Winn (Eds.), *Humanizing research: Decolonizing qualitative inquiry with youth and communities* (pp. 223–248). Sage.

Waling, A. (2018). I can't/can I touch him? Erotic subjectivity, sexual attraction, and research in the field. *Qualitative Inquiry*, *24*(9), 720–727. https://doi.org/10.1177/1077800417734561

Webber, V., & Brunger, F. (2018). Assessing risk to researchers: Using the case of sexuality research to inform research ethics board guidelines. *Forum Qualitative Sozialforschung/Forum: Qualitative Social Research*, *19*(3). https://doi.org/10.17169/fqs-19.3.3062

5

"OUT OF AFRICA"

Critical reflexivity as decolonial method?

Introduction

In a moment that Nelson Maldonado-Torres (2017) terms the "decolonial turn" in psychology, psychologists are increasingly reflecting upon possibilities for decolonising our research methods and practices. Critical psychologists from the Global South continue to be key contributors to conversations around developing methodology for decolonial inquiry and intervention in psychology (see e.g. Bhatia, 2017; Boonzaier & van Niekerk, 2019; Canham, 2018; Kessi, 2018; Macleod et al., 2020; Manganyi, 2019; Ratele, 2019). It is within this moment that this chapter turns to the following question: what do we do when we find our own research about stigmatised sexual practices operates in ways that reproduce the colonial subject positions we aim to challenge and subvert through our research?

Questions about how race and racist discourses operate in men's talk on paying for sex are relevant to all research about men who pay for sex, and certainly in the post-apartheid, post-colonial South African moment in which these interviews took place. Nevertheless, relatively little critical qualitative research explicitly addresses how race informs men's constructions of paying for sex (Huysamen & Boonzaier, 2018). In this chapter, I apply intersectionality and feminist decolonial theories to further build on the critical reflexive approach I have outlined in this book. I use this historically informed approach to interrogate how vectors of power such as race, class, gender, and

DOI: 10.4324/9781003093602-5

sexuality operated together within the interviews to shape the meanings produced there. I provide excerpts from interviews to demonstrate how men deployed racist and colonial discourses to manage and defend against the stigma associated with sex work in South Africa. I examine how my positionality as a white women researcher made racist and colonial discourses utterable in the interviews and explore the possibilities for using critical reflexivity as a tool for decolonial research practice.

Applying intersectionality and feminist decolonial theories to critical reflexive practice

Intersectionality theory contends that people's gendered identities will always overlap with their other social identities, for example, race, class, sexuality, religion, disability, and age, in dynamic and complex ways. These various social categories cannot be understood as separate from one another, but rather as interlocking systems of oppression that work together to maintain the oppression of some and the dominance of others (Collins, 1990; Crenshaw, 1991).

As a researcher working around the social issues of gender, sexuality, and disabilities in both South Africa and the United Kingdom, I am repeatedly struck by how the lives of the people I do research with just *are* intersectional (Boonzaier et al., 2020). What I mean is, rather than the compartmentalising, the "specialising in", narrowing down, or filtering out that is characteristic of much academic theory and practice, thinking intersectionally is a commitment to seeing and giving voice to what is always-already there. It is writing, theorising, and thinking about complex lives, lived all at once through the modalities of race, class, disability, gender, and sexuality. Therefore, thinking intersectionally is as much an undoing of theory as it is a doing of theory. Thinking intersectionally involves understanding how race, class, gender, sexuality, and disability are articulated through and by one another and operate to produce the subjects that we write and theorise about.

I follow critical feminist psychologist Floretta Boonzaier (Boonzaier, 2017; Boonzaier et al., 2020; Stephens & Boonzaier, 2020) who employs feminist decolonial theory to understand gendered relations in post-colonial post-apartheid South Africa. Feminist decolonial theory goes beyond understanding various categories or vectors of power as intersecting and argues for an understanding of these structures as fused and indiscernible from one another (Lugones, 2007). For example, from a feminist decolonial perspective, gender is always-already racialised and racism and neoliberalism are always-already gendered (Gill, 2008; Rutherford, 2018). Decolonial theory looks at how the dehumanised and infantilised black "Other" was manufactured through the process of colonisation and how these colonial representations of the black Other continue to be produced and reproduced today. Lugones (2007) articulates that gender, and gender hierarchies, cannot be understood outside of colonisation and coloniality because colonisation involved a twofold process of racial inferiorisation and gendered subordination. As Boonzaier and I have written elsewhere,

> A feminist decolonial reading is sensitive to the ways in which the bodies of the gendered, racialised and classed Other have been manufactured and continue to be produced and reproduced, sometimes in new, imaginative and insidious ways and sometimes in ways that are no different to its colonial production.
>
> *(Huysamen & Boonzaier, 2018, p. 61)*

Applying intersectionality and feminist decolonial theory to inform our critical reflexive research practice means going beyond the researcher listing their social identities and positionality and acknowledging, in a lonely paragraph, that these might influence the research. It includes but goes beyond viewing interview encounters as places where researchers are committed to bearing witness and giving voice to our participants' lives lived at the intersections of these vectors of power. As decolonial researchers, we commit ourselves to employing research methods and practices that humanise our participants and the researcher and aim to make the research encounter more egalitarian (Matutu, 2019). Employing this kind of critical reflexivity implies being willing to explore how the interview encounter – even where decolonial research practices have been employed – is not immune to these interlocking systems of oppression. It involves being willing to constantly ask how the gendered, racialised, and classed Other might, in particular moments, be produced and reproduced *within* our interviews and through our research. Lugones (2010, p. 746) suggests that, "unlike colonization, the coloniality of gender is still with us; it is what lies at the intersection of gender/class/race as central constructs of the capitalist world system of power". The kind of critical reflexivity that I advance in this book calls for us, as reflexive feminist decolonial researchers, to be willing to interrogate the ways in which the coloniality of gender is still with us, right here, in our research interviews.

To commit oneself to doing decolonial research practice is to acknowledge that histories of slavery, imperialism, and colonialism are always-already infused with the contemporary social issues we seek to understand today (Gqola, 2010). Taking the time to learn about how these longstanding systems of oppression have operated over time in relation to the issues we study will assist in understanding how they have manifested today in our participants' contemporary experiences of the world and how they might play out in our interviews.

Research in psychology is often guilty of taking an ahistorical approach to social enquiry. We arrive at research questions about people's experiences of "contemporary" social issues or practices (like HIV self-testing, online porn consumption and production, pelvic mesh surgery, or chemsex) without taking the time to trace the origins of these or related practices and the complex social meanings and histories with which they are entangled. We develop surveys, we use experimental designs, or develop interviews to answer research questions in ways that do not allow us to connect these contemporary issues to their deeper histories.

Chapter 1 presents a snapshot of the ways in which sex work has historically been associated with dirt and disease, and its links to constructions of class, providing deeper understanding of how the stigma surrounding sex work operates. Learning about the longstanding colonial discourses around sex work, contagion, and black women's bodies helped me to recognise and more meaningfully interpret these discourses in my participants' contemporary narratives. I was interested to explore the relationship between sex work and HIV, specifically how sex workers have been constructed as "at risk" and "risky" bodies in terms of the HIV epidemic in South Africa. Delving into historical accounts of sex workers, disease, and risk, I quickly found that social anxieties around the connections between sex work and the spread of sexually transmitted disease is not a contemporary issue. Similar discourses can be found in colonial legal and medical discourses.

The extent to which one might go to produce historically informed research depends on the researcher's interests and resources. Producing more historically informed research questions could involve conducting a thorough review of literature (secondary sources) that provides historical accounts of the social issue we study. In terms of sex work,

I have found the work of Gilman (1985a, 1985c), Levine (2003), and Van Heyningen (1984) invaluable. However, as critical psychologists, our research practice could be further enriched if we were to develop our own skills by building an archival or historical element into our research design. If I were to conduct this study again, I would spend time at the National Archives in London to look at colonial legal papers and the National Archives in Pretoria to examine post-colonial papers. I might also conduct a discourse analysis of representations of sex workers in local newspapers over time. The British Library, for example, holds copies of all issues of the *Cape Times*, first published in 1876 and still in circulation today. It would be fascinating to conduct a discursive analysis to see how sex workers' bodies have been represented in this publication, and how this changed over time.

Discourses of disease: the intersections of gender, race, and class in men's talk about paying for sex

Men who pay for sex in South Africa, and indeed in most locations across the globe, do so amidst pervasive and longstanding discourses of dirt, disease, and contagion associated with sex work. These associations of disease are connected with fear and elicit moral panic in many societies (Joffe, 1999). By participating in the study, men automatically implicated themselves in a deeply stigmatised activity that poses potential threats to their identity in terms of their cleanliness, respectability, and class. As Berthold (2010) suggests, "dirt, contamination, or pollution are labels likely to be associated with behaviours that fall outside of, and thereby *threaten*, our most carefully guarded categories of social classification, including races, classes, genders, and sexualities". Participants arrived to interviews as *defended subjects* with identities (fathers, husbands, businessmen, respected community members) to protect against the potentially stigmatising discourses of dirt, disease, and moral corruption associated with sex work. How did men manage and negotiate their identities in relation to the stigma associated with paying for sex? In this chapter I attend to this question.

Splitting sex workers

The most common way men defended against stigmatising associations between sex work and dirt and disease was to split women into two kinds of sex workers: either the dirty and diseased sex worker or the clean and "classy" sex worker. Polarised representations of women either as all-good or all-bad, pure or promiscuous, dirty or clean, are neither new nor unusual, and can be traced back as far as ancient Greece (Bareket et al., 2018). Freud (1905) was the first to name this process when he articulated the Madonna–Whore complex. Contemporary research shows that this dichotomous construction of women's sexuality remain dominant in men's talk today and serve to reinforce hetero-patriarchal gender relations (Bareket et al., 2018; Bernstein, 2018; Hollway, 2001; Huysamen & Boonzaier, 2015; Seal & Ehrhardt, 2003).

Participants achieved this binary distinction between dirty and clean sex workers by constructing sex workers who operated on the streets as essentially different to those who worked from indoor contexts. They described street-based sex workers as dirty, cheap, disease-ridden, and morally corrupt. Conversely, sex workers operating from indoor venues were deemed physically clean and hygienic, more respectable, and "classier" than women who sold sex on the street. By splitting sex workers into clean and dirty women, the morally corrupt and the respectable, men were able to establish boundaries between themselves and the "dirty" category of sex workers, with 37 out of the 43 of the participants stating that they would never patronise street-based sex workers.

Simpson et al. (2012, p. 2) assert that "cleanliness is about establishing boundaries, separating the pure from the contaminated and imposing a system on an 'inherently untidy experience'". This rings true in the following quote where Steve classifies or ranks sex workers within a hierarchical "three-tiered system":

> And then, so it seems there are three tiers, at least. You've got the street-workers and over here they are plentiful. Dodgy. Dodgy because of diseases, dodgy because of crime, dodgy because half of them rip people off. Then you've got the agency kind of tier, brothel . . . And you see the ads, the newspapers and the websites. And then there's the really, really classy [private] women, amazing. And I almost, I almost admire them for their detachment from conventional values and their courage and their, um, I guess, I don't know really how to put it, but their uniqueness.
> *(Steve, 57, white: Face-to-face)*

Steve's narrative clearly illustrates the intersection between dirt, disease, gender, and class. The cleanliness and classiness of the private sex worker is emphasised through juxtaposition with the dirty and diseased street-based sex worker. In addition to constructing private sex workers as "classy", as opposed to "dodgy" and diseased, Steve describes them as having different moral standards. While street-based sex workers are viewed as criminals and likely to "rip people off", the "really classy" women are described in terms of respectability, as having some kind of moral high ground, as he explains that he admires their "detachment from conventional values" and their "courage". This idea of respectability is important because, as Skeggs (1997) suggests, respectability is a key signifier of class. This is an example of how notions of dirt and disease come to symbolise moral dirt or decay, and how physical purity acts as a proxy for moral purity and respectability.

Similarly, Hoang (2011) found that wealthy Vietnamese men paid what they defined as beautiful "high-end" Vietnamese sex workers for sex as a way of asserting their class and status in public. This was also tied into notions of dirt and disease, as one participant in Hoang's study stated, "I don't go to those low-class dirty girls, you know? These girls are young and pretty, and other men want them" (Hoang, 2011, p. 390). Both my and Hoang's interview data highlight how participants' use of discourses of dirt and disease versus cleanliness and respectability are important for negotiating social class, which in turn allows men to command a position of power and status in relation to other men. By producing the category of the clean and respectable "upper class" sex worker, distinctive from the dominant stigmatised understandings of the diseased "lower class" sex worker, men were able to distance themselves from the dirty and diseased Other and position themselves as clean and respectable by association.

Producing the Other

Joffe (1999, p. 14), in her work on people's responses to risk, argues that understandings of disease are connected with fear and collapse. However, "people do not hold on to this fear. Rather, they externalise it. Once located outside of the self the fear is removed and it is the 'other', rather than the self who faces catastrophe". Building on Joffe's work around producing the Other as a response to risk, I argue that this process of Othering is useful to understand how people manage stigma as a threat to identity. Paying for sex in South Africa is associated with stigma that threatens one's identity. However, my research shows that people do not always hold on to that stigma, they externalise it. Once located outside of the self, the stigma is removed and it is the Other, rather than the self who faces this stigma.

The concept of the Other is useful for exploring the discursive mechanisms participants employed to manage and defend against threats to their identities and anxieties this elicits. Stuart Hall (2001) articulates the crucial role that the Other plays in the negotiation of identity. He suggests that the process of identification is not only based purely on identifying with a particular group, but it is also about disidentifying with the Other:

> Identity means, or connotes, the process of identification, of saying that this here is the same as that, or we are the same together, in this respect. But something we have learnt from the whole discussion of identification, in feminism and psychoanalysis, is the degree to which that structure of identification is always constructed through ambivalence. Always constructed through splitting. Splitting between that which one is, and that which is the other.
>
> *(Hall, 2001, p. 146)*

According to Hall, producing the Other is crucial for establishing one's identity – my interview data suggest that it is also crucial for defending it. In the following excerpt, we see how the production of the Other operates to allow Anesh to construct his identity favourably:

ANESH: I used to laugh. I used to. Men who went for pavement specials [laughing] they got a kick out of parking their Audi A8 in Voortrekker Road and having this hideous hooker. I mean hideous, I mean hideous where you swear this woman has got AIDS. She's got like, you know what I mean?
MONIQUE: Yea, yea
ANESH: But one thing I can tell you, pavement specials: no, no.

(Indian, 40: Skype)

In much the same way as Steve describes street-based sex workers as "dodgy" and diseased, Anesh expresses an almost visceral disgust for the street-based sex worker. He associates her with "AIDS" and hatefully describes her as a "hideous hooker". The term "pavement special" is a colloquial term used in South Africa to describe a mixed breed or mongrel dog. Thus, when Anesh calls the woman who sells sex on the street a "pavement special", he dehumanises her. Anesh also establishes his superiority over, and distance from, the kind of men who pay for sex on the street by describing himself gazing upon and laughing at them. Anesh's narrative does more than just produce the Other dirty and diseased sex worker, it also produces the Other client. This allows him to position himself not only in terms of cleanliness and respectability but also as *superior* to other stigmatised men who pay for sex on the street.

In this excerpt, Anesh looks to me to recognise and confirm his description of this kind of woman by saying, "you know what I mean?" There is an implicit assumption here that I would recognise his description and, even as a woman myself, I would understand the woman he describes as Other. He felt safe enough to speak freely like this in the knowledge that I would agree with him rather than be offended by his dehumanising description of another woman. And we see that I oblige him. Was this a missed opportunity to challenge this dehumanising description of the Other as it was reproduced in the interview? Or had I provided Anesh with a safe platform to tell me what he was really like? Or was it both? I further explore these research quagmires later in the chapter.

The intersections of race and class with discourses of dirt and disease

> Cleanliness and dirt are accordingly inscribed onto particular bodies, affording them different levels of value.
>
> (Simpson, 2007, p. 7)

Participants' descriptions of street-based sex workers as lower class, dirty, and diseased were also entangled with notions of race, with only certain bodies – black bodies – constructed as dirty and diseased. Conversely, white bodies were imagined as clean and as holding a high value. The following conversation between Cyril and myself illustrates these intersections of race, class, and gender:

CYRIL: If it was, if it was an upper-class situation. If it was middle class and below, I would have a problem with it.
MONIQUE: So, what would the difference be?

CYRIL: Okay, the difference would be, and now it's becoming a racial thing. Okay. The upper-class people will not sleep with another colour. And I'm talking about, there's two ex-Miss South Africa's that are in this game. Okay. Alright and it's categorically stated okay that they do not entertain other races, okay. So that is the, that is the bottom line of that scenario. Where, where whereas if it's middle to sort of lower, okay, that is: wham, boom, bang, you just pay. . . . It's not a, it's not a racial thing, okay not at all, absolutely not at all. It is a thing of risk. That is the biggest thing. Okay, because, because the amount of people that are out of Africa that are in Cape Town at the present moment in time. I mean there is all types of diseases that come with it. And I'm not talking, I'm not talking sexual, I'm not talking STD, I'm not talking sexual diseases. I'm talking diseases as in *diseases*. You know like Ebola and stuff like that, that a person doesn't know. So, so it is it is a very sort of . . . huge risk factor.

MONIQUE: As in you feel that those diseases are attached to people of colour more than to white people?

CYRIL: Ja, because of the situations.

MONIQUE: And by situations?

CYRIL: The areas, ja the areas ja, that they come from. I mean if you go in, I mean if you go up into Africa, it's riddled. It's riddled with all types, all types of things. You know? . . . I'm not being discriminatory. It's not a colour issue. (53, white: Face-to-face)

Cyril distinguishes clearly between sex workers who are "upper class", "middle" class, and those who are "below" middle class. What is particularly striking is how explicitly and candidly Cyril confounds class and race. In no uncertain terms, he constructs "upper class" in terms of whiteness and "lower classes" in terms of blackness. However, Cyril does not refer directly to race by using the terms "white" or "black". Rather he uses "upper class" as a signifier for whiteness and allows "lower class" to stand in for blackness. Moreover, he takes it for granted that I do too. It is only because of our shared whiteness, and because of an *assumed* shared understanding that "upper class" means whiteness, that "other colour" or "other races" could hold this meaning in our conversation. Similarly, when I ask Cyril to elaborate on why he associates disease with black people, his justification is "because of the situations". Again, Cyril assumes there is a shared knowledge or common consciousness between us. Cyril does not feel he has to explicate what the "situations" in "Africa" are, because he assumes that, as a function of my whiteness, I already know. It is because of mine and Cyril's shared whiteness that the black Other is so easily produced within this interview. Similarly, a participant named Johan (48, white, face-to-face) said, "white people, we, we know the context around it. I'm very realistic about the economy and what is happening in South Africa". Johan's remark again reflects this assumption that as "white people", *we* had a collective understanding about race in South Africa. My presence as white interviewer made interviews a safe and comfortable context for participants like Cyril and Johan to express their racism.

Cyril specifically clarifies his statements about black bodies and diseases by saying "I'm not talking STD, I'm not talking sexual diseases. I'm talking diseases as in *diseases*. You know like Ebola". This statement clarifies that in this conversation he is not just associating black sex worker's bodies with stigmatised notions of sex work (as responsible for the spread of sexually transmitted diseases), but rather that he is drawing on a racist discourse of black bodies as generally diseased and contagious. His unwillingness to have sex with black sex workers or any woman who has sex with black men is underpinned by a colonial assertion that black bodies are germ carriers and white bodies are vulnerable to contamination by black bodies (Gilman, 1985b; Levine, 2003; Zoia, 2015). This close *proximity* to black bodies is seen to pose a danger for white bodies (Berthold, 2010; Levine, 2003).

Cyril employs a discourse of disease to sanction his own racism. He repeatedly uses language like "if you go up into Africa" and "people that are out of Africa". He uses these discursive mechanisms to create distance between himself and the black people he is describing. He draws on the colonial trope of black bodies coming from distant locations "out of Africa" as diseased (Jungar & Oinas, 2004). This also reproduces the colonial invention of Africa as a singular place with a uniform set of pathologies (Mudimbe, 1988). Spronk (2014) argues that this notion of a unified "Africanness" has been used in scholarly work to produce degrading essentialist constructions of black masculinity. The notion of "African men" is a mechanism of Othering, one that is "premised upon a historical process of Western imagination and practices where Africa served as the paradigm of difference" (Spronk, 2014, p. 515).

Sara Ahmed's work on *orientation* is pertinent to participants' imaginaries of black bodies being "out of" or "up into" Africa. Ahmed

(2006) theorises that since colonial times, whiteness has been maintained and reproduced though both its proximity to other white bodies and through its distance from black bodies:

> The alignment of race and space is crucial to how they materialize as givens, as if each "extends" the other. In other words, while "the other side of the world" is associated with racial "otherness", racial others become associated with the "other side of the world". They come to *embody distance*. This embodiment of distance is what makes whiteness "proximate" as the "starting point" for orientation. Whiteness becomes what is "here", a line from which the world unfolds, which also makes what is "there" on "the other side of the world".
>
> *(Ahmed, 2006, p. 121)*

Ahmed claims that distance is what defines racial Otherness. Distance from the racial Other defines and maintains whiteness. Similarly, Ahmed suggests that closeness ("what is here") comes to define whiteness and racial sameness. Whiteness must, therefore, be reproduced through intimate proximity to white bodies. Consequently, too much proximity with blackness threatens this reproduction of whiteness. Cyril was not the only participant to use this kind of health/disease discourse to validate their racism and to establish racial difference between their white bodies and Othered "diseased black bodies". Nine out of the 11 participants I interviewed face-to-face openly said that they would not have sex with black women. A further 11 out of the 32 men I interviewed online stated the same. Following are some examples of how this racist rhetoric ran through participants' narratives:

> Mm, I wouldn't, I wouldn't go black. I wouldn't go foreign, as in Malawi.
>
> *(Peter, 50, white: Face-to-face)*

> I'll be honest, ah white and coloured girls only.
>
> *(Mark, 38, Indian: Face-to-face)*

> I haven't met one [black woman] in my life that was really of interest.
>
> *(Piet, 55, white: Face-to-face)*

I won't go to someone that say, "all races welcome". Specifically, someone who qualifies it and it's only whites. You limit certain risk with that.

(Johan, 48, white: Face-to-face)

I know issues can be with any person, but I never will go to a black . . . health issues with AIDS and stuff.

(Ashish, 37, Indian: IM)

I don't want to cross the racial barrier . . . I don't want, say someone who knows me and sees me to go around and tell everybody that guys sleeps with blacks.

(Gideon, 53, white: IM)

Black women in general, though one shouldn't generalise. But there's something about the skin or the smell or the something, it just er, doesn't reach me.

(Steve, 57, white: Face-to-face)

Participants' repeated association of the black body with dirt, disease, and risk are no coincidence. They reflect a long history of racism in South Africa, stemming from colonisation. Chapter 1 presents a more detailed discussion on the role of discourses of contagion in producing black bodies as subjugated Other while valorising and sanitising the white colonists in colonial South Africa. Zoia (2015, p. 158) argues that,

> Occurring at a time when the British Empire was at its zenith, it would be the black body that was to assume the role of principal germ-carrier, for the white colonists could certainly not blame their (imagined to be) superior selves for epidemic disease.

Constructions of black bodies as dirty and diseased are alive and well in democratic South Africa today. These discourses still operate to maintain the status of black bodies as less desirable than white bodies and continue to filter through into people's gendered identities. In South Africa, these perceptions are given public and scientific legitimacy though biomedical HIV/AIDS discourses. Patton (1990) has written about the idea of "African AIDS" as instrumental in broader public understandings of black bodies as diseased. Colonial constructions of black sexuality were revived in efforts to explain the characteristics of the AIDS epidemic during the 1980s (Patton, 1990). Similarly, Spronk (2014), in their critical paper on how academic research on male sexuality in Africa has produced degrading notions of black masculinity, shows how colonial racism has been incorporated into Eurocentric academic discourses. Likewise, Jungar and Oinas (2004), in their analysis of various texts about HIV/AIDS prevention (both scientific and media), show how these texts also construct HIV/AIDS as an African problem and African men as "high risk" for HIV/AIDS and other diseases. These assumptions are both based on and reproduce "colonial imaginations of 'African sexuality'" (2004, p. 97).

The doubleness of discourse in racist narratives about sex work

What do men's descriptions of black bodies as dirty and diseased "do" in these interviews? Hall (2001, p. 147) writes about the "doubleness of discourse", suggesting that identity is always composed of more than one discourse, and that for every narrative about a black body there is an (at times) unspoken, corresponding narrative about a white body. In other words, the discourses of the dirty black body present in participants' narratives were simultaneously discourses about whiteness. Talk of dirty black bodies did as much for white bodies as it did for black bodies. Just as the relationship between class and discourses of dirt and disease serves to defile and degrade the black body, so it idealises the white body (Berthold, 2010). In thinking about the meaning the white body has (only) in relation to the black body, Fanon's (1986, p. 146) words remain pertinent:

> When one is dirty one is black – whether one is thinking of physical dirtiness or of moral dirtiness. It would be astonishing, if the trouble were taken to bring them all together, to see the vast number of expressions that make the black man the equivalent of sin . . . Blackness, darkness, shadow, shades, night, the labyrinths of the earth, abysmal depths, blacken someone's reputation; and, on the other side, the bright look of innocence, the white dove of peace, magical, heavenly light. A magnificent blond child – how much peace there is in that phrase, how much joy, and above all how much hope!

Constructions of the black Other were a necessity for the white men's negotiation of their own masculinities in interviews. Cyril's articulation of the black Other as a lower class, dirty, disease-carrying body coming from "out of Africa" is significant not only in how it constructs blackness but also by what it "does" for whiteness. By imagining Other black bodies as lower class and diseased, he is able to position his own white body as the opposite, as higher class and disease free. In this way, Cyril can distance himself from any associations of disease that may be attached to his identity as a man paying for sex in the context of South Africa. The distant black Other from "out of Africa" allows Cyril to position himself in terms of idealised whiteness, rather than through the lens of what society deems the "dirty" practice of paying for sex.

The idealised white body: proximity to whiteness and internalised racism

The preceding section demonstrates how white bodies were idealised and black bodies were denigrated and shamed in men's narratives about paying for sex. However, it was not only white men who drew on these racist discourses. Some Indian and the black participants also negotiated desirable identities for themselves by splitting sex workers into dirty and clean women and by drawing on racist understandings of white bodies as pure and disease-free. The excerpt that follows is taken from an interview with Riedwaan, who described himself as a "traditional Indian" man. Riedwaan was one of the very few participants who said that he patronised street-based sex workers. In this excerpt, we see how Riedwaan defends against the discourses of dirt and disease associated with street-based sex workers by distancing himself from black bodies and describing himself as having sex with clean white bodies:

RIEDWAAN: I think it also comes from the standards I've set for myself. I wouldn't pick just anybody up. I mean, cleanliness is something that is important to me. Safety is something that is important to me. So, at the end of the day even if you were in the mood to pick someone up, for example, I could drive around for half an hour before I decide on who . . . Someone who was actually, I mean who firstly you trust to actually pick up. They not going to get in and want to rob you and steal from you. From a safety in terms of health obviously, in terms of diseases.

MONIQUE: Okay. But how would you know?

RIEDWAAN: It's difficult to obviously assess . . . I suppose it's the same rule of thumb that you apply to day-to-day life. We mix with people who we assimilate with. . . . In the sense that if you meet someone for the first time and argument's sake you've got relatively good hygiene yourself and the other person doesn't, mm you wouldn't judge them by it, or at least I wouldn't, but I probably wouldn't want to hang out with them as often. And I think that's something which I set for myself and that's the reason, again I don't want to sound racist but if you in Joburg, you found a black girl on the street, chances are she wouldn't be that clean. So you'd probably prefer a white woman, in terms of Joburg. And that's the other reason why I'd rather go to Boksburg. Because you would find more white women available.

(Riedwaan, 32, Indian: Face-to-face)

Riedwaan's narrative is clearly about identity management, as he defends his identity against the discourses of dirt and disease associated with paying for sex on the street. To do this, Riedwaan describes himself in terms of a health and sanitisation discourse, using words like "cleanliness" and "hygiene". To evidence his own cleanliness, he describes how he avoids "dirty women" when selecting which sex workers to have sex with. I ask Riedwaan how he would be able to know by looking at someone whether they had diseases. He explains that they should appear to have the same level of hygiene as himself and that they should not be black, because if he were to find a black sex worker on the street, the "chances are she wouldn't be clean". Just like many other participants, he equates black bodies to dirt and disease. Riedwaan juxtaposes the black body with the white body by saying "so you would probably prefer a white woman". Zoia (2015, p. 17) suggests that "to say something is clean is to imply that other things are dirty; people hold both ends of the binary in mind, whichever is being invoked at any point in time". Riedwaan did not need to explicitly describe the white body as clean and disease free; in fact, he did not describe the white body at all. This extra clarification would have been redundant, because the black body has already done the discursive work (by virtue of its "dirtiness") in constructing the white body as clean. Again we see how Hall's notion of the *doubleness of discourse* is relevant (2001, p. 147). By having sex with a white body, orientating himself closely to the white body and as far from the black body, Riedwaan can construct his own body as clean and respectable. These interviews also provide striking examples of how racism is internalised by black and Indian participants and manifests in their lives. In interviews with black and Indian participants, whiteness and lightness of skin tone are championed above other racial identifications, including their own, maintaining the discourses of the idealised white body and the denigrated black body. An example of how internalised racism operates is evident in the following excerpt. To provide some context, this section of talk is part of a longer conversation where Anesh articulates why he prefers paying white and fair-skinned women for sex. He starts by explaining why choosing white or fair women as sexual partners is important for his identity. Here Anesh is referring to an ex-fiancé who is also Indian but has a very light complexion. Anesh told me he remained unmarried, despite wanting a wife, because all the Indian women he met subsequently were either too short or "too dark".

ANESH: Uh no, no, no, look for me it was look, look on the screen you can see, I'm a dark individual. My ex-fiancée, she was fair, like you, she was white. She was white, she was tall, she was everything that I was looking for, you know? . . . After her I met weird, the girls were either too short, too dark. I mean look seriously, I'm a dark man. I want a fair woman. I don't want my kids Bournville[1] chocolate sorry [laughs] really seriously, you will only be seeing their teeth. I come from a community where the dark Indians tell their kids you marry the fair ones, you know? And the fair ones tell them you marry the fair ones because we don't want dark kids in the family.
MONIQUE: Wow, that's quite hectic
ANESH [Laughing] You know, for me, I mean really for me for me it was also like status for me, you know what I mean? It was status for me, because you know you want a fair person. You know you don't want a, I know it's being sectionist. We were, I can use the word, in my home community we were racist.

(40, Indian: Skype)

Initially, I had difficulty understanding Anesh's discrimination of Indian women based on skin tone or complexion. I wrote in my research journal, "I'm struggling to understand why the shade of another Indian person's skin would be this crucial to Anesh that he'd rather be alone than be with a dark-skinned woman". This journal entry reflects my ignorance and my privileged position as a white woman. Unlike Anesh, I have never had to think about the tone of my own skin, beyond simply being "white". It is so much a part of my taken for granted reality that I have not had to consider how the shade of my skin would make me closer to, or further from, being white, and thus more or less desirable or powerful in a society that continues to value and privilege white bodies over black bodies. My journal entry is also reflective of my ignorance concerning how racism operates not only across different racial identities but also within them through colourism[2] and internalised racism, permeating all relations, interactions, practices, and discourses.

What is central to this narrative is Anesh's acknowledgement of his own darkness within a community that devalues dark skin. It is through this internalised racism, this internalised antiblackness that Anesh's preference for light-skinned women can be understood. The women's lightness "does" something for Anesh's darkness: he explains that having a fair-skinned woman as his wife would afford him the "status" that his community associates with light skin. As Ahmed (2006) suggests, whiteness must be reproduced through intimate *proximity* to white bodies. Anesh constructs light-skinned women as valuable to him, because by marrying a light-skinned woman he is more likely to produce light-skinned offspring. Anesh's narrative, and his disdain for dark-skinned women shows how gender cannot be understood outside of race and racial inferiorisation, and similarly how race cannot be understood outside of gendered hierarchies (Lugones, 2007). Anesh expresses his perception of the worthlessness of dark-skinned women through his distaste at the thought of having dark-skinned children, with skin like "Bourneville" dark chocolate, saying, "You will only be seeing their teeth". This powerful imagery suggests that when whiteness is contrasted with darkness, the only part that will be "seen", or perhaps matters, is the whiteness. Not only would his offspring be more valued and desirable within his community if they were lighter, but also he, as a man, would command a higher status, and be more respected and powerful, if he produced light-skinned children. Thus, a light-skinned woman is valued as a sexual partner because she does something for Anesh's masculinity. Anesh's masculinity, his value as a man in his society, is articulated through racialised sexual relations. Anesh's masculinity is articulated through his proximity to light-skinned women's bodies (Ahmed, 2006).

Both Riedwaan and Anesh's narratives show how the notion of orientation and the proximity of white bodies to black bodies can provide important insights to how some men negotiate the meanings of paying for sex (Ahmed, 2006). Both men value the ways in which paying for sex allow them to associate themselves with, and come into close proximity to, desirable and idealised white bodies as a way of negotiating respectability, class, affluence, and, therefore, power (Ahmed, 2006). Men's desire to pay to have sex with light-skinned sex workers cannot be understood in isolation from broader cultural, racial, economic, and social factors because this desire for light bodies, and men's paying to be in close proximity to them, is heavily tied up with power and status and colonial constructions of otherness versus sameness (Ahmed, 2006).

The researcher's positionality and the coloniality of gender in the interview

I return to the question of my positionality and its implications for the researcher–participant dynamics. Was I implicated in Anesh's story about his failed relationship and the tensions between cultural expectations, masculinity, and respectability? Indeed, I was. Anesh introduces his story about gendered race relations by positioning himself in terms of darkness and me in terms of whiteness. On our video call, he demands that I acknowledge the difference that exists between us by saying, "look on the screen you can see, I'm a dark individual" and "she was fair, like you, she was white". Even in online video interviews, we remain embodied researchers and participants. In this moment, I become the idealised white woman and he becomes the denigrated black body. It is in relation to my white body that Anesh articulates his beliefs around the worthlessness of dark women's bodies. Anesh's narrative powerfully illustrates how racist colonial discourses are reproduced and come alive within the interview context and in this moment, I am faced with the reality that the coloniality of gender is with us, right here in our research encounters.

Concluding thoughts: methodology as pedagogy and praxis

Pattman and Bhana (2009, p. 212) suggest that identity is constructed through producing the racial or gendered Other "which becomes a fantasy structure into which difference is projected, a peg onto which fears or desires can be hung". This chapter has presented an analysis of the process of constructing an Other onto which the stigma of paying for sex can be placed. Men deploy racist colonial tropes to construct the black body as lower class, dirty, and diseased to manage their anxieties and the threats to their identities owning to the continued stigmatisation of sex work. I have demonstrated how my body, coded for respectability as a young, white, and educated woman, made the interview context fertile ground for the co-production of this colonial fantasy of the Other. This research serves as a striking example of how, as Ratele and Shefer suggest, "intimate relations continue to be a key site for the reproduction of racism and binaristic discourses of 'us' and 'them' in contemporary South Africa" (Ratele & Shefer, 2013, p. 190).

I share Twine's sentiment when they say, "I hope that field researchers and ethnographers, even those whose research is not specifically concerned with racial disparities, will consider the significance of race as a methodological issue" (Twine, 2000, p. 5). This chapter has highlighted the importance of approaching race as a methodological issue when doing research around gender and sexuality. It speaks to the complex intersection between race, class, gender, and sexuality, and reminds those of us who primarily research gender and sexuality of how deeply and inextricably these will always already be infused with race and class (Collins, 1990; Lugones, 2007). When I embarked on this project, I was aware that participants' narratives about their gender and sexualities might be intersected by discourses of race and class. However, I had not foreseen that discourses of race and colonial fantasies of the Other would be quite so dominant and fused with their narratives about gender and sexuality. This presented me with an example of what Lugones (2007) calls the "coloniality of gender" in action. Ratele and Shefer (2013), writing about the *Apartheid Archive Project*, reflect on how the narratives they collected coalesced around gender and sexuality despite them not explicitly asking participants about gender-related issues. My research has shown how the inverse is equally true: when asking people about gender and sexuality, constructions of race and class are likely to emerge consistently because these systems of oppression are inextricable from one another.

Butler (1999, p. 78) also encourages us to ask questions such as "how is race lived in the modality of sexuality?" and "how is gender lived in the modality of race?" Questions such as these, if we ask them in and of our research, become tools to help us grasp and capture the fused nature of these systems. I have stressed the value of situating ourselves as researchers within this critical intersectional reading of our interview data. Throughout this book, I have demonstrated why it is methodologically, theoretically, and ethically imperative that we acknowledge the impact that we as researchers have on the research process by employing a critical reflexivity to our analysis. In this chapter, I have illustrated how men's narratives were riddled with racist colonial discourses that functioned to degrade black bodies as well as valorise and privilege white bodies. But how did I as the researcher contribute to the racist rhetoric that ran through these interviews? While these are difficult and painful questions to explore, they are possibly some of the most important questions that this book has addressed. Regardless of how "open-ended" our research questions are, or how neutrally we believe that we position ourselves, our interviews always allow for the telling of certain stories and the silencing of others.

My presence as a white middle-class woman enabled the telling of certain racist narratives within the interviews. Because of my whiteness, participants felt that they could, quite comfortably, construct the black body as Other in my presence. In some instances, I even got the sense that participants' racist narratives were actually *for* me. I have written elsewhere (Huysamen, 2016) about how participants attempt to position themselves as "good" and "respectable" men in interviews about paying for sex. For example, in the current study, I got the sense throughout Johan's interview that he was trying to describe his paying for sex in ways that he thought would reassure me of his respectability. In the early stages of an interview with Johan he said, "I'm not saying I do this twice a week . . . you tend to go to someone that is fairly clean, I'm very cautious about that . . . and that you know it's only a specific race". For Johan, just like minimising how frequently he paid for sex, assuring me that he did not have sex with black people was one way he thought he could make himself more respectable in my eyes. Similarly, Duneier (2000), a white male researcher writing reflexively about his ethnographic research with street vendors in New York, reflects on how a white businessman he spoke to during his field work was explicitly racist and extremely derogatory about black street vendors. Duneier suggests that the white businessman felt comfortable using racist language in his presence because he considered Duneier to be a racial insider, and thus assumed that they shared an understanding about these black men. Duneier reflects on how, if he were a black researcher, he would have been unlikely to collect such racist narratives during his fieldwork. Similarly, I must question whether, if I were a black woman, these interviews would have elicited the same narratives. Is it likely that men would have been able to look me in the eyes and describe my body as disease carrying and dirty? Although I cannot answer these questions with complete certainty, what is certain is that there were moments where my white body invited, symbolised, and sanctioned racism within these interviews.

My identity as a white middle-class woman was intimately implicated in the data produced within the interviews and it went on to shape how they were interpreted and written up. I have demonstrated how my white body, coded for respectability, sanctioned and sometimes even invited racist discourses. But what are the implications of knowing that our interviews provide a context where racist fantasies can be imagined, uttered freely, and sometimes spoken into being to produce the Other in the moment of the interview? What are we to do with the knowledge that we will inevitably collude with our participants through our work, or reproduce the very discourses we are trying to resist? It begs the question: should white bodies be doing research about black bodies? Although I have no definitive answers to these questions, what I do know is that colonial, racist, and patriarchal constructions will trickle down into any social research we do, regardless of the topic. Both the interviewer and the participant will inevitably "do" race, class, gender, and sexuality there. Rather than denying that these dynamics exist in our research, we should design our analysis to recognise and acknowledge them. This will allow us to harness the possibilities that the interview context provides for learning about how these dynamics operate, as well as equip us with the skills to better manage them in the future.

A research design that requires the researcher to reflect critically on their own positionality facilitates a process whereby the researcher becomes more aware of how these systems of power and oppression operate both within the interview and outside it. For example, by engaging in this kind of intersectional critical reflexivity, I more fully understood how my own privilege as a white woman operated. Perhaps some white people's "difficulty" in acknowledging our privilege lies partly in how we choose to define privilege. We often equate the term privilege to financial wealth and access to various resources and opportunities. However, the critical reflexive work done in this project shows how the privilege and power that white bodies wield is linked to more than just wealth and opportunity. Through participants' polarised constructions of black and white women's bodies, and in realising that my body had become implicated in these narratives, I fully grasped that because I am a white woman I am positioned as more respectable, valued, and desirable within society. It seems strange that I had not fully comprehended this, and that it took the analysis of my positionality within an interview context, as an "ah-ha" moment, to allow me to do so. However, as Duneier (2000) suggests, it is often in that which we take most for granted that we find the greatest examples of our own privilege.

Employing this critical reflexive approach to our research is thus, in and of itself, pedagogic and generative. Engaging with the research process and data at this level has the potential to allow us as researchers to develop more critical understandings of how these vectors of power operate in society. The interview acts as a microcosm where we can witness first-hand how the theories of power and oppression that we study unfold in practice. Employing this critical reflexive approach, and training new researchers to do so, is also a matter of research ethics and integrity and one form of decolonial research practice. It helps researchers to become more sensitive to these dynamics when they do play out in our interviews. It allows us to be more aware of how the gendered, racialised, and classed Other comes to be produced *within* our interviews and through our research. This equips and prepares us to respond to our participants and to our research in more thoughtful and astute ways that could better resist these damaging discourses and make room for the imagining of alternative and more empowering ones.

Notes

1 A brand of dark chocolate.
2 *Colourism* can be defined as an internalised form of racism, often amongst people within the same ethnic group, which involves prejudice, stereotyping, and perceptions of beauty according to the lightness or darkness of one's skin, whereby lightness of skin colour is valued and privileged over darkness of skin (Burton et al., 2010; Gabriel, 2007). Colourism does not exist independently of racism, but rather colourism can be seen as a product or "fundamental building block" of racism and white supremacy (Hunter, 2005, p. 2).

References

Ahmed, S. (2006). *Queer phenomenology: Orientations, objects, others.* Duke University Press.

Bareket, O., Kahalon, R., Shnabel, N., & Glick, P. (2018). The Madonna-Whore dichotomy: Men who perceive women's nurturance and sexuality as mutually exclusive endorse patriarchy and show lower relationship satisfaction. *Sex Roles, 79*(9), 519–532. https://doi.org/10.1007/s11199-018-0895-7

Bernstein, W. M. (2018). *A basic theory of neuropsychoanalysis.* Routledge.

Berthold, D. (2010). Tidy whiteness: A genealogy of race, purity, and hygiene. *Ethics & the Environment, 15*(1), 1–26.

Bhatia, S. (2017). *Decolonizing psychology: Globalization, social justice, and Indian youth identities.* Oxford University Press.

Boonzaier, F. (2017). The life and death of Anene Booysen: Colonial discourse, gender-based violence and media representations. *South African Journal of Psychology, 47*(4), 470–481. https://doi.org/10.1177/0081246317737916

Boonzaier, F., Huysamen, M., & van Niekerk, T. (2020). Men from the "South": Feminist, decolonial and intersectional perspectives on men, masculinities and intimate partner violence. In L. Gottzén, M. Bjørnholt, & F. Boonzaier (Eds.), *Men, masculinities and intimate partner violence.* Routledge.

Boonzaier, F., & van Niekerk, T. (Eds.). (2019). *Decolonial feminist community psychology.* Springer. https://doi.org/10.1007/978-3-030-20001-5

Burton, L. M., Bonilla-Silva, E., Ray, V., Buckelew, R., & Hordge Freeman, E. (2010). Critical race theories, colorism, and the decade's research on families of color. *Journal of Marriage and Family, 72*(3), 440–459.

Butler, J. (1999). *Bodies that matter: On the discursive limits of "sex".* Routledge.

Canham, H. (2018). Theorising community rage for decolonial action. *South African Journal of Psychology, 48*(3), 319–330.

Collins, P. H. (1990). *Black feminist thought: Knowledge, and the politics of empowerment.* Hymann.

Crenshaw, K. (1991). Mapping the margins: Intersectionality, identity politics, and violence against women of color. *Stanford Law Review*, 1241–1299.

Duneier, M. (2000). Race and peeing on sixth avenue. In F. W. Twine & J. W. Warren (Eds.), *Racing research, researching race: Methodological dilemmas in critical race studies* (pp. 215–226). New York University Press.

Fanon, F. (1986). *Black skin, white masks.* Pluto Press (Original work published 1952).

Freud, S. (1905). Three essays on the theory of sexuality (1905). In *The standard edition of the complete psychological works of Sigmund Freud volume VII (1901–1905): A case of hysteria, three essays on sexuality and other works.* www.pep-web.org/document.php?id=se.007.0123a

Gabriel, D. (2007). *Layers of blackness: Colourism in the African diaspora.* Imani Media Ltd.

Gill, R. (2008). Culture and subjectivity in neoliberal and postfeminist times. *Subjectivity, 25*(1), 432–445. https://doi.org/10.1057/sub.2008.28

Gilman, S. L. (1985a). Black bodies, white bodies: Toward an iconography of female sexuality in late nineteenth-century art, medicine, and literature. *Critical Inquiry, 12*(1), 204–242.

Gilman, S. L. (1985b). Black bodies, white bodies: Toward an iconography of female sexuality in late nineteenth-century art, medicine, and literature. *Critical Inquiry, 12*(1), 204–242.

Gilman, S. L. (1985c). *Difference and pathology: Stereotypes of sexuality, race, and madness.* Cornell University Press.

Gqola, P. D. (2010). *What is slavery to me?: Postcolonial/slave memory in post-apartheid South Africa.* Wits University Press; JSTOR. https://doi. org/10.18772/12010045072

Hall, S. (2001). Old and new identities, old and new ethnicities. In L. Back & J. Solomos (Eds.), *Theories of race and racism: A reader* (pp. 144–154). Psychology Press.

Hoang, K. (2011). "She's not a low-class dirty girl!": Sex work in Ho Chi Minh City, Vietnam. *Journal of Contemporary Ethnography, 40*(4), 367–396.

Hollway, W. (2001). Gender difference and the production of subjectivity. In M. Wetherell, S. Taylor, & S. J. Yates (Eds.), *Discourse theory and practice: A reader* (pp. 272–284). Sage.

Hunter, M. (2005). *Race, gender, and the politics of skin tone.* Routledge.

Huysamen, M. (2016). Constructing the "respectable" client and the "good" researcher: The complex dynamics of cross-gender interviews with men who pay for sex. *NORMA: International Journal for Masculinity Studies, 11*(1), 19–33.

Huysamen, M., & Boonzaier, F. (2015). Men's constructions of masculinity and male sexuality through talk of buying sex. *Culture, Health & Sexuality, 17*(5), 541–554.

Huysamen, M., & Boonzaier, F. (2018). "Out of Africa": Racist discourse in men's talk on sex work. *Psychology in Society, 57*, 58–80.

Joffe, H. (1999). *Risk and "the other".* Cambridge University Press.

Jungar, K., & Oinas, E. (2004). Preventing HIV? Medical discourses and invisible women. In S. Arnfred (Ed.), *Re-thinking sexualities in Africa* (pp. 97–114). Nordic Africa Institute.

Kessi, S. (2018). Photovoice as a narrative tool for decolonization: Black women and LGBT student experiences at UCT. *South African Journal of Higher Education, 32*(3), 101–117. https://doi.org/10.20853/32-3-2519

Levine, P. (2003). *Prostitution, race, and politics: Policing venereal disease in the British Empire.* Routledge.

Lugones, M. (2007). Heterosexualism and the colonial/modern gender system. *Hypatia, 22*(1), 186–219.

Lugones, M. (2010). Toward a decolonial feminism. *Hypatia, 25*(4), 742–759.

Macleod, C. I., Bhatia, S., & Liu, W. (2020). Feminisms and decolonising psychology: Possibilities and challenges. *Feminism & Psychology, 30*(3), 287–305. https://doi.org/10.1177/0959353520932810

Maldonado-Torres, N. (2017). Frantz Fanon and the decolonial turn in psychology: From modern/colonial methods to the decolonial attitude. *South African Journal of Psychology*, *47*(4), 432–441. https://doi.org/10.1177/0081246317737918

Manganyi, C. N. (2019). *Being-black-in-the-world*. Wits University Press.

Matutu, H. (2019). "On the way to calvary, I lost my way": Navigating ethical quagmires in community psychology at the margins. In *Decolonial feminist community psychology* (pp. 111–128). Springer.

Mudimbe, V. Y. (1988). *The invention of Africa: Gnosis, philosophy, and the order of knowledge*. Indiana University Press.

Pattman, R., & Bhana, D. (2009). Colouring sexualities: How some black South Africans schoolgirls respond to "racial" and gendered inequalities. In M. Steyn & M. Van Zyl (Eds.), *The prize and the price: Shaping sexualities in South Africa* (pp. 21–38). HSRC Press.

Patton, C. (1990). Inventing "African AIDS". *New Formations*, *10*, 25–39.

Ratele, K. (2019). *The world looks like this from here: Thoughts on African psychology*. Wits University Press.

Ratele, K., & Shefer, T. (2013). Desire, fear and entitlement: Sexualising race and racialising sexuality in (re)membering apartheid. In G. Stevens, N. Duncan, & D. Hook (Eds.), *Race, memory and the apartheid archive* (pp. 188–207). Palgrave Macmillan.

Rutherford, A. (2018). Feminism, psychology, and the gendering of neoliberal subjectivity: From critique to disruption. *Theory & Psychology*, *28*(5), 619–644. https://doi.org/10.1177/0959354318797194

Seal, D. W., & Ehrhardt, A. A. (2003). Masculinity and urban men: Perceived scripts for courtship, romantic, and sexual interactions with women. *Culture, Health & Sexuality*, *5*(4), 295–319.

Simpson, A. (2007). On ethnographic refusal: Indigeneity, "voice" and colonial citizenship. *Junctures: The Journal for Thematic Dialogue*, *9*.

Simpson, R., Slutskaya, N., & Lewis, P. (2012). Introducing dirty work, concepts and identities. In *Dirty work: Concepts and identities*. Palgrave Macmillan.

Skeggs, B. (1997). *Formations of class and gender*. Sage.

Spronk, R. (2014). The idea of African men: Dealing with the cultural contradictions of sex in academia and in Kenya. *Culture, Health & Sexuality*, *16*(5), 504–517.

Stephens, A., & Boonzaier, F. (2020). Black lesbian women in South Africa: Citizenship and the coloniality of power. *Feminism & Psychology*, *30*(3), 324–342. https://doi.org/10.1177/0959353520912969

Twine, F. W. (2000). Racial ideologies and racial methodologies. In F. W. Twine & J. W. Warren (Eds.), *Racing research, researching race: Methodological dilemmas in critical race studies* (pp. 1–34). New York University Press.

Van Heyningen, E. B. (1984). The social evil in the Cape colony 1868–1902: Prostitution and the contagious diseases acts. *Journal of Southern African Studies*, *10*(2), 170–197. https://doi.org/10.1080/03057078408708077

Zoia, F. T. P. (2015). *Sanitizing South Africa: Race, racism and germs in the making of the apartheid state, 1880–1980* [Doctoral dissertation, Indiana University]. http://gradworks.umi.com.ezproxy.uct.ac.za/37/02/3702579.html

6

USING THE CRITICAL REFLEXIVE APPROACH IN YOUR RESEARCH

Introduction

A central aim of this book, and the critical reflexive approach it introduces, has been to provide researchers with a set of tools to systematically build reflexivity into every phase of the research process. The hope is that researchers will do this not only because it is methodologically important, but because they recognise that it is theoretically generative too. Each chapter has demonstrated how this critical reflexive approach helped me to collect rich, detailed data and aided me in building textured, nuanced, historically informed understandings of men's motivations for paying for sex and of the complex ways in which they managed their identities around this stigmatised practice. I hope that this research approach will be as fruitful to other researchers working on topics of a sexual, stigmatised, or secret nature as it has been to me.

The nine elements of the critical reflexive approach

The critical reflexive approach is not a step-by-step research guide. While this book does not provide a formula, it does provide a lens. It offers an assemblage of theories, assumptions, values, priorities, and principles that together shape how we view the research encounter and how we approach and interpret the knowledge that is produced

DOI: 10.4324/9781003093602-6

there. The elements set out in the pages of this book can be used flexibly to assist the researcher to build an approach to critical reflexivity that is tailored to suit their unique research questions, participants, and processes. Following are nine of the core elements that together make up the foundations of the critical reflexive approach.

1 Research arrivals

Research is about arrivals of various kinds (Sandberg, 2011). The critical reflexive approach requires the researcher to attend to these arrivals at every stage of the research process. Attending to arrivals in research is a commitment to taking nothing about our research process for granted. It involves acknowledging that everything about our research is the way it is because of a particular set of decisions, historical events, and discursive meanings. It is about documenting these decisions, histories, and discursive forces, and using this to better understand our research encounters and the data that are produced there.

Researchers do not just do research about sexual or stigmatised topics; we arrive at our research topics. Practicing critical reflexivity involves acknowledging that we have arrived at our specific research questions (and not others that have been either discounted or not thought of). It involves exploring our reasons for arriving. And it involves acknowledging that we arrive to our research with our own assumptions and anxieties around the research encounter and the stigmatised topics we study. As Chapter 2 demonstrates, behind every research question, participant recruitment strategy, data collection tool, and method of data analysis are a set of decisions that have been made by the researcher. These decisions create a set of possibilities and impossibilities for the research encounter; therefore, the researcher is already implicated in the data that will be produced in the future research encounter. Practicing critical reflexivity is investigating the implications that our research decisions may have on the research process and using this to inform how we interpret and represent our research data.

Our participants do not just magically become our research participants; they arrive to our research. They arrive to the research encounter with their own anxieties, hopes, and expectations. A key element of the critical reflexive approach is theorising our participants as arrivals to our research and, specifically, exploring why they have arrived.

It is also about acknowledging the inverse, that some people do not arrive, and interrogating what implications these non-arrivals have on our research findings. As Chapter 3 demonstrates, investigating why our participants arrive to our research can provide valuable insights into how they make meaning of the topics and practices they arrive to discuss, while also offering insights into the complex interviewer–participant power dynamics at play within research encounters.

2 Careful eclecticism

Theoretical eclecticism underpins all aspects of my critical reflexive approach to research. This places value on transgressing the borders of theoretical approaches through careful adaptation and combination (Gavey, 2011). Rather than adhering to just one theoretical framework, or one approach to the stories our participants tell during interviews, the critical reflexive approach encourages the researcher to assemble a collection of theories, principles, and philosophies that together will allow them to build critical reflexivity into the research process. While this does not require a specific combination of theories and methodologies, it does require the researcher to select theoretical approaches that allow them to attend to the productive or constructive nature of language and its relationship to power (Foucault, 1981; Parker, 2004). It requires the researcher to work with theories and approaches that together allow them to stand back and look at the broader social structures that shape the meanings and subject positions produced in interviews and beyond, as well as to zoom in to examine the finer interpersonal dynamics and individual anxieties that operate within each interviewer–participant relationship. As noted in Chapter 2, this book draws on an assemblage of poststructuralist and psychoanalytic theories and practices. Placing these theories and practices carefully in conversation with one another provides the theoretical foundations and the methodological tools necessary to interrogate how both interpersonal dynamics and broader social structures shape interview encounters and captures how these manifest and are reproduced in the interview to shape the data that are produced there.

3 Theorising the interview as a social encounter

The critical reflexive approach theorises the interview as a social encounter, one that is not immune to the interpersonal dynamics and social structures that operate in other kinds of social encounters. It is to assume that, just as we "do" gender, sexuality, race, and class in our everyday lives, both interviewer and participant "do" their various intersecting social identities within the interview encounter (West & Zimmerman, 1987). From a critical reflexive approach, the interview is not understood as a place where people's stories and accounts are merely extracted, but a place where identities are actively performed, negotiated, and produced (Ahmed, 2006; Butler, 2008). Theorising the interview in this way involves accepting the impossibility of neutrality within the research encounter and understanding meaning as co-produced by both interviewer and participant.

Approaching the interview as a place where identity is performed and produced means that all the interactions between interviewer and participant, including those which may fall outside of what is usually deemed to be interview data (like pulling out a chair or insisting on paying a bill) become part of the research data. All the non-verbal communications, silences, and interviewer–participant dynamics *are* the data, meaning that the volume of data collected in each interview is considerably denser. This has implications for how data are transcribed, as it is essential within this approach that the interview transcripts capture all these nuances and dynamics.

4 Defended subjects

The critical reflexive approach assumes that both the researcher and the participant will arrive to research encounters as *defended subjects* (Hollway & Jefferson, 2013). This is to assume that the researcher and participant will perceive some threat to their identities within the interview encounter, eliciting anxieties that they will defend against in the interview. The theory of the defended subject assumes that people draw on particular available discourses and discursive positions rather than others as defences against feelings of anxiety and as a way of managing their identities (Hollway & Jefferson, 2013). Theorising the interviewer and participant as defended subjects is particularly valuable in research about stigmatised practices and desires around which people feel shame and anxiety, as through their engagement in the research both the researcher and participant will implicate themselves in these stigmatised practices, and thereby feel threats to their identities.

The critical reflexive approach is committed to attending to the ways in which these anxieties and defences operate in the interview and how they work to facilitate shape and restrain the data that are produced there. As Chapter 4 demonstrates, the researcher's own defences will have an impact on the research, for example, on which kinds of sexual stories are invited and which are silenced. Interrogating how anxieties and defences operate within the interview relationship provides a deeper understanding of participants' subjectivities, guards against superficial readings of the data, and offers an opportunity to interrogate the complex and shifting power dynamics at play within the research encounter.

5 Sexual subjects

The critical reflexive approach calls for understanding both researchers and participants as sexual subjects. This is simply a commitment to acknowledging what is already there. It involves recognising that interviews about sex can evoke sexual feelings, emotions, physiological responses, anxieties, and desires in both participants and researchers. It also involves accepting that this does not delegitimise the research, nor does it negate the integrity of the researcher. Further, this contains a commitment to resisting the pressure to misrepresent our interviews and wholly neutral and sanitised spaces. Finally, it involves building a critical awareness and thoughtful analysis of these sexual dynamics into the research process so that we can ethically manage these elements, learn from them, and support other researchers to do the same.

6 Producing the Other

Another valuable tool used in the critical reflexive approach is identifying when and how the Other is produced within our participants' narratives. The central assumption is that the production of the Other is a form of identity management (Hall, 2001). People's identities are threatened by association with stigmatised practices or discourses, and this elicits anxieties. But we do not hold onto this anxiety; rather, we find ways to distance ourselves from the stigma and to displace it onto an Other (Joffe, 1999). The Other is a useful concept when researching topics of a stigmatised nature, as it allows researchers to pinpoint where the threats of stigma are felt, to understand how participants manage and negotiate this stigma, and indeed how we ourselves might become implicated or complicit in these productions. It can be a helpful data analysis tool: when you spot moments in interview transcripts where the Other is produced, you are almost sure to find that stigmatising issues that pose threats to identity are being discussed, and that identities are being managed and defended there.

7 An intersectional approach to the research encounter

This book has highlighted the importance and pedagogical value of approaching race as a methodological issue when doing research around gender and sexuality. Taking an intersectional approach to sex research is to acknowledge that research about sex and sexuality is already and always research about gender, about race, about class, and about disability (Boonzaier et al., 2020). An intersectional approach encompasses a commitment to giving voice to our participants' narratives about sex in their entirety, as they are intersected and infused with other aspects of their identities and positionalities, rather than homing in on our research agendas and questions. Chapter 5 reflects on how racial and class identities operate and are reproduced within the interview relationship, and how these dynamics offer important insights into the ways that our participants make meaning of their sexual experiences and negotiate their sexual identities. The critical reflexive approach requires the researcher to situate themselves within intersectional readings of the interview data, and to examine the ways that their own gendered, racialised, and classed bodies are deeply implicated in which narratives can be told and which become unspeakable.

8 A historically informed approach to the research

Taking a historically informed approach to our research involves attending to yet another kind of arrival. Linked to the intersectionality agenda, this involves a commitment to tracing the origins of the social issues and practices we study to understand the complex social meanings and histories with which they are entangled. Often, the sexual practices and identities that are stigmatised, criminalised, or considered taboo in contemporary society are complicated by histories of colonialism, imperialism, patriarchy, homophobia, and capitalism, which shape how they are understood in the present. A historically informed approach encompasses a commitment to develop research methods and practices that allow us to connect the contemporary issues we study to their deeper histories to better understand how these have an impact on the data produced in the interview encounter and on our participants' lives. Crucially, as demonstrated in Chapter 5, this requires a commitment to reflect on how we as researchers may be implicated in these histories. It requires us to examine how we may reproduce tired gendered tropes or harmful colonial discourses through our research practices and responses so that we can begin to develop better ways of doing research that recognises and resists these interconnected legacies of oppression.

9 The research journal as research tool and data

The final, and perhaps the most important, element of the critical reflexive approach is the researcher's reflective journal. This is where we see many of the other elements in action. Here, the researcher captures their thoughts, responses, observations, and anxieties in relation to the research process. They also record and reflect on any aspects or moments in the research encounter that they feel are important but may otherwise be lost in transcription. The researcher records their thoughts and reflections during all phases of the research process, from when they start to design their study, when they apply for ethical approval, through to when they analyse the data, and perhaps still when they disseminate the findings.

There are no requisites for the format of the journal: it could be a handwritten journal, a digital journal, an audio journal, or a combination of these. The only necessity is that the researcher's reflections are recorded consistently and systematically throughout the research process. When taking a critical reflexive approach, the research journal is not an added extra, it is a central part of the research process, and a tool for embedding reflexivity into every phase of the research. During the data analysis phase, each interview transcript is analysed alongside the corresponding journal entries for that research encounter. The reflexive accounts recorded in the research journal assist the researcher to contextualise and interpret the data, but they also become the research data. This kind of reflexive approach is not conducted as an aside, separate from the rest of the analysis. It is an inseparable part of the analysis, woven into the very fabric of the methodological approach.

Concluding thoughts

These are the nine foundational elements of the critical reflexive approach. Together they have assisted me to develop an approach to research that foregrounds questions of power within the interview relationship and interrogates the researcher's role in shaping the knowledge that is produced there. They will, I hope, also assist other researchers working on topics of a sexual, stigmatised, or secret nature to do the same. This methodological approach offers ways of using reflexive practice to theoretical ends: to build better understandings of our participants' stories and deeper insights into their subjectivities, as well as the broader social practices that our research sets out to explore. I hope that other researchers will draw on these elements of the critical reflexive approach with the intention of not only making their research more ethical, rigorous, and transparent, but also generating better data and new theoretical insights.

References

Ahmed, S. (2006). *Queer phenomenology: Orientations, objects, others*. Duke University Press.

Boonzaier, F., Huysamen, M., & van Niekerk, T. (2020). Men from the "South": Feminist, decolonial and intersectional perspectives on men, masculinities and intimate partner violence. In L. Gottzén, M. Bjørnholt, & F. Boonzaier (Eds.), *Men, masculinities and intimate partner violence*. Routledge.

Butler, J. (2008). *Gender trouble: Feminism and the subversion of identity*. Routledge.

Foucault, M. (1981). *The history of sexuality, volume I: An introduction*. Penguin Books (Original work published 1976).

Gavey, N. (2011). Feminist poststructuralism and discourse analysis revisited. *Psychology of Women Quarterly, 35*(1), 183–188.

Hall, S. (2001). Old and new identities, old and new ethnicities. In L. Back & J. Solomos (Eds.), *Theories of race and racism: A reader* (pp. 144–154). Psychology Press.

Hollway, W., & Jefferson, T. (2013). *Doing qualitative research differently: A psychosocial approach* (2nd ed.). Sage.

Joffe, H. (1999). *Risk and "the other"*. Cambridge University Press.

Parker, I. (2004). Discourse analysis. In U. Flick, E. Kardorff, & I. Stein (Eds.), *A companion to qualitative research* (pp. 308–312). Sage.

Sandberg, L. (2011). *Getting intimate: A feminist analysis of old age, masculinity and sexuality* [Doctoral dissertation, University of Linköping]. http://liu.diva-portal.org/smash/record.jsf?pid=diva2:408208

West, C., & Zimmerman, D. H. (1987). Doing gender. *Gender and Society, 1*(2), 125–151. https://doi.org/10.2307/189945

INDEX